GOOD HOUSEKEEPING

MICROWAVE
COOKING
For One or Two

GOOD HOUSEKEEPING

MICROWAVE

COOKING

For One or Two

EBURY
PRESS

Published by Ebury Press
Division of The National Magazine Company Ltd
Colquhoun House
27–37 Broadwick Street
London W1V 1FR

First impression 1986

ISBN 0 85223 421 X (Paperback)
0 85223 436 8 (Hardback)

Editor: Gill Edden
Design: Peter Bridgewater Associates
Illustrations: Annie Ellis
Photography: Paul Kemp
Stylist: Jane Kemp
Cookery: Janet Smith

Cover photograph: Seafood Pasta (page 76)
Plate kindly loaned by the Craftsmen
Potters' Association shop

Computerset by MFK Typesetting Ltd, Hitchin

Printed in Great Britain at
the University Press, Cambridge

CONTENTS

INTRODUCTION	6
BREAKFAST	14
LIGHT MEALS FOR ONE	24
SNACKS	34
LUNCH	44
MAIN DISHES	60
DINNER FOR TWO	80
ACCOMPANIMENTS	94
DESSERTS AND CONFECTIONARY	104
GLOSSARY	117
INDEX	126

INTRODUCTION

THE ADVANTAGES OF MICROWAVE COOKING IN A SMALL HOUSEHOLD

MICROWAVE COOKING offers advantages to everyone, but particularly to people who live in small households of one or two people as it is especially suited to dealing with small quantities of food quickly, easily, cheaply and cleanly.

Many larger households tend to use a microwave cooker as a back-up to a conventional oven. But microwave cooking know-how has now become so advanced, technically and gastronomically, that it is possible to cook a wide variety of foods successfully from scratch by this method. So a microwave cooker is not useful just for thawing and reheating convenience foods. It is an important cooking tool for business couples with little time to spend at the cooker, for people who live alone and couples whose children have left home, for students who need to cook in a bed-sitter and for disabled people for whom conventional cookers and kitchen design present insuperable problems. A microwave cooker can be sited on a shelf or trolley of convenient height anywhere it is comfortable to work.

SPEED of cooking is important for anyone who leads a busy life or doesn't want to spend hours in the kitchen, and microwave cookers are especially good at cooking small quantities of food very fast indeed. Unfortunately, with this cooking method – unlike conventional cooking – the more you cook, the longer it takes, so when preparing microwaved food for a crowd you may end up with little time saving. But for one or two people, even the most complicated dishes are likely to require less than 15 minutes cooking time.

Microwave cooking is *simple* – once you know how. It is, however, a different technique from conventional cooking and you cannot except to master it immediately. It should be treated as something you need to learn and understand, and which will take practice before you achieve good results. As with any new subject it makes sense to start by cooking things that are straightforward, and to develop your techniques as and when you are ready. For example, it is difficult to accept, if you are used to a conventional oven, that a matter of a few seconds too many or too few can be critical in preparing a dish.

ENERGY SAVING is rarely out of the news these days and most people are keen to keep their fuel bills as low as possible. Microwave cookers run off a 13 amp socket outlet and cost only a few pence per hour to run on full power. Since they are used for only short bursts of power they offer a considerable saving over cooking in a conventional oven. If you feel guilty at the thought of switching on a full-size oven at high heat just to thaw a flan for two or bake a single potato, a microwave will solve your problem.

CLEANLINESS is a big plus with microwave cooking. Because the walls of the cooker do not get very hot, food does not burn on to them as it does in a conventional oven. A microwave cooker is easily cleaned just by wiping around the inside with a damp cloth if anything has spilled. In any case most microwave cooking is done with the food covered so that there is little chance of spattering.

SMELLS in the kitchen too are much less when cooking by microwaves. The short cooking time and method of cooking do not produce fumes and steam, so the kitchen does not need powerful ventilation.

A microwave cooker is a *compact* appliance. Even the largest model will sit comfortably on a work surface (or trolley if you want to move it from room to room) and the very small models are still large enough to cook food in reasonable quantities (they will take a 2 kg/3½ lb chicken) and occupy very little space if kitchen quarters are cramped.

HOW MICROWAVES WORK

THE FIRST POINT to make is that microwave cooking is *safe*. The actual microwaves are non-ionising, short wavelength, high frequency waves which do not build up in the body in the way that ionising X-rays and gamma rays do. In any case, microwave cookers are built to high safety standards with several interlocks on the door to keep the rays where they belong – inside the oven and penetrating the food. When buying a microwave cooker look for models which carry the BEAB (British Electro-technical Approvals Board) safety label which is a guarantee that the cooker has been manufactured and tested to the highest safety standards. When cooking, the electrical energy produced when the cooker is plugged into a 13 amp socket outlet is transformed into indirect voltage which is then converted by a fuse called a magnetron into the microwaves. These pass through materials such as glass, china, plastic, paper, wicker and wood, and penetrate food. They vibrate the water molecules in food, billions of times a second, producing the heat which carries out the cooking process.

Short wavelength rays penetrate and cook the food

Shield thin parts of food with smooth foil, shiny side in

Microwaves cannot pass through metal, so metal containers should not be used for microwave cooking as they deflect the rays and affect the working of the cooker, possibly damaging the magnetron to a point where the cooker no longer works. However, it is safe to use very small, smooth pieces of kitchen foil to protect less dense parts of food which would otherwise cook more quickly than the thicker parts.

Microwaves can penetrate food to a depth of about 5 cm (2 inches) and because of the way they are directed into the cooker cavity they enter the food on all sides. With food that is more than 10 cm (4 inches) thick, cooking is done by a 'knock on' effect whereby heat from the vibrating molecules gradually penetrates the whole area. You will note that some of the recipes in this book specify a standing time after cooking in the microwave. This is to allow full penetration of the heat since cooking continues after the power is switched off. It is important to adhere to the recommended standing time or you may find that food is undercooked.

Microwaves do not brown foods and many people feel the need to overcome this problem. You can, of course, use a conventional grill to finish off dishes or you can buy a combined microwave/convection oven which incorporates radiant heat for browning. Browning dishes are also available (see page 117) for use within the microwave cooker itself.

COOKERY TECHNIQUES

Turning food manually may be necessary

Because microwave cookers vary in power output it is sensible to start by using the cookery book supplied by the manufacturer as this will be designed for your particular model. However, there are some general rules which should be followed when cooking by microwave:

♦ Most cookers incorporate either a stirrer or paddles which distribute the microwaves around the oven cavity, or a turntable which rotates the food so it is penetrated evenly by the microwaves. If the cooker appears to have hot spots, *turn the food manually during cooking time.*

♦ Cooking time depends on the density of the food and its starting temperature. Thin pieces of food will cook quicker than thick ones, and those at refrigerator or room temperature more quickly than frozen food.

♦ Where possible food should be cut into evenly sized pieces to ensure even cooking.

♦ When cooking evenly-sized pieces of food (eg meatballs) it is important to move those at the outside – which cook faster – into the middle so that all the pieces are done at the same time.

♦ Because the outer edges of food tend to cook first, either stir food in the middle of cooking time or turn it. When arranging food to be cooked, place the thicker parts at the outer edge of the cooking container.

♦ Try to leave a space in the middle of the food so that microwaves can penetrate from the inner as well as outer edges. Ring moulds are useful for this, or you can put a tumbler in the middle of a dish.

♦ Fatty foods tend to spatter so cover with a piece of absorbent kitchen paper.

♦ Food, apart from baked goods, should be kept moist. Either use cling film, which should be pierced or folded back a little to allow steam to escape, or a lid.

♦ Foods which have not been covered while cooking should be covered with foil during standing time to keep the heat in.

If you haven't got a ring mould, use an empty tumbler to provide a central space in the food

♦ Food which has a skin (tomatoes, potatoes, liver) needs to be pricked before cooking so that pressure does not build up inside and cause an explosion.

♦ Fat and sugar attract microwaves and get hot before other ingredients. Beware of things like jam in the middle of a doughnut or filling in a sweet pie as these can be considerably hotter than the rest of the dish.

♦ Start cooking meat with the fat side down and turn it halfway through cooking if more than 5 cm (2 inches) thick.

♦ Salt toughens meat, fish and vegetables and makes them dry out. It is best to add it after cooking.

♦ Wipe out the cooker with a damp cloth after spills. If the interior of the cavity smells after cooking something like fish or cabbage, place a bowl of water with a little added lemon juice in the cooker and microwave on HIGH for a minute. The resulting condensation can be wiped off with a clean cloth and the smell should disappear.

All foods with a skin should be pricked before cooking

THAWING & REHEATING

THERE ARE MANY people who use their microwave cookers only for thawing and reheating foods and these are indeed important functions. Thawing requires skill in terms of timing, especially with foods that do not require further cooking; there is no problem in thawing a casserole which is to be reheated, but something like a terrine which is to be served cold needs exactly the right amount of power to produce a successful result. Reheating too is a matter of timing – not critical on certain dishes but important with others. Follow the instructions exactly and do not forget to allow standing time.

MICROWAVE COOKWARE

YOU WILL FIND that much of your standard cookware is suitable for microwave use provided that it is not metal. Watch out though for items which are decorated with gold or silver, which could deflect microwaves, and for certain types of earthenware which may contain metal particles. Materials like glass and china work well in microwave cookers but in general the best materials are those designed specifically for microwave use and which will transmit microwave energy as efficiently as possible.

To check how good a container is at transmitting microwave energy, carry out the following test. Half fill it with water and microwave on HIGH for 1 minute. If the water is hot and the top of the container remains cool, the microwaves are passing through efficiently. If both the water and container are warm the container can be used but it will take longer to cook the food as more microwaves are trapped in the material of the container. If the water is cool and the container hot, the majority of the microwaves are being trapped in the container material and it is not an efficient container for microwave cooking.

The shape of your cookware is important because of the patterns in which the microwaves move around the oven cavity. Round containers are preferable to square ones as they have no corners in which clusters of microwaves can concentrate, overcooking the food at these points. Straight sides to containers are more efficient than sloping ones, which cause food at the shallower outer edge to cook more quickly.

Shallow containers cook food more quickly than deep ones as the food has a greater surface area over which to spread, but a deep container should be your choice if you *want* to cook food more slowly. Dishes should in general be larger than when cooking in a conventional oven; food with lots of liquid will tend to bubble up when hot, and baked foods rise more during cooking than they would in a standard oven.

Small containers are suitable for individual portions; either use ceramic ramekins or buy from the special ranges of microwave ware. These come in long-lasting, semi-disposable and disposable forms. Semi-disposables can be re-used serveral times provided they are washed carefully. Disposables should only be used once and then with care. Some of the board type suitable for conventional ovens become floppy when filled with a hot liquid and may become too hot to handle if used with food which contains a lot of fat or sugar.

In addition to a reasonable number of small containers (quite a lot if you want to freeze meal-sized portions for one or two people) you will need cling film for wrapping and covering foods and roasting bags for cooking poultry and joints of meat. Always use a plastic tie or rubber band to seal a roasting bag as metal ones deflect the microwaves and cause arcing (ie sparking), which may damage the cooker. Note that microwaved food is very hot when removed from the cooker so take care not to scald your hands when taking off a cover or cling film. Although microwaves do not heat containers in the same way that conventional cooking does, the parts of the container which are in contact with food will become very hot and oven gloves should be used. Small containers in particular tend to get hot so be sure you have the kind of oven gloves which are not too rigid to grasp a ramekin.

Take care not to scald yourself

BROWNING

MICROWAVE COOKERS cannot brown foods unless they also incorporate some form of convection heating. Only items which are cooked for a long time – a whole chicken, for example – will become brown; chicken pieces, sponge puddings, shepherd's pie and other small items will have pallid tops. To achieve browning you can either put the dish under a conventional grill, or you can disguise the pale colour with other foods – paprika on chicken pieces, icing on cakes. For many foods you can use a special browning dish which is coated with a substance which heats up quickly when exposed to microwaves and provides a hot surface which will sear items like sausages, chops and chicken pieces.

MICROWAVES FOR ALL MEALS

BREAKFASTS are something that a microwave cooker does supremely well. The microwaved breakfast could include individual mugs of coffee or tea with the water boiled directly in a mug. Rolls or croissants can be warmed through in a matter of seconds. Butter (removed from any protective foil) can be given a small burst of power to produce spreading consistency. Cooked dishes can be prepared quickly. Scrambled or poached eggs take only a minute or so but don't try to boil an egg or it will explode. Always prick the yolk of an egg which is poached or cooked *en cocotte* to prevent pressure building up inside the membrane and causing it to explode. Bacon and sausages are best cooked on a browning dish, covered with kitchen paper to prevent spattering. Dishes like kedgeree and porridge reheat well and can be eaten from their cooking dishes to save washing up. Crystallised honey or golden syrup will return to normal if microwaved on HIGH for 1–2 minutes with any metal lids removed. If necessary transfer the required amount to a serving dish. Frozen bread thaws quickly – one slice takes about 10–15 seconds on LOW, plus 2 minutes standing time; a whole large sliced loaf takes 6–8 minutes on LOW and needs 15 minutes standing time.

L UNCH for the small household also benefits from microwave cooking and the fuel saved by not putting on a full-sized oven to heat up something like an individual frozen pizza or a slice of quiche. A bowl of soup can be heated and eaten immediately with a warm roll, and leftovers – often staple lunchtime fare for those at home – can be warmed up without drying out. Microwaving is particularly good for this type of cooking, allowing food not only to retain moisture but also texture; a far cry from the wizened portions of reheated stew that tend to emerge from a conventional oven.

D INNER as a full-scale meal for one or two is easily prepared from scratch in a microwave cooker. Several small items can be cooked at once, but if the cooking times vary, simply calculate the times required and cook accordingly. Elaborate, time-consuming dishes take only minutes to cook, making dinners for one or two just as quick, and more exciting, than convenience foods. Instant dinners need no planning if you freeze food in individual portions for reheating when needed.

HOW TO USE THE RECIPES
IN THIS BOOK WITH YOUR OVEN

UNDERSTANDING POWER OUTPUT AND OVEN SETTINGS

e.g. *Medium* (60%)
= %Power × Total Number
of Settings on Oven
÷100=Correct Setting
i.e. $=\dfrac{60\times9}{100}=5$

Low (35%)
= %Power × Total Number
of Settings on Oven
÷100=Correct Setting
i.e. $=\dfrac{35\times9}{100}=3$

UNLIKE CONVENTIONAL ovens, the power output and heat controls on various microwave ovens have yet to be standardised. When manufacturers refer to a 700-watt oven they are referring to the oven's POWER OUTPUT; its INPUT, which is indicated on the back of the oven, is double that figure. The higher the wattage of an oven, the faster the rate of cooking, thus food cooked at 700 watts on full power cooks in half the time as food cooked at 350 watts. That said, the actual cooking performance of one 700-watt oven may vary from another with the same wattage because factors such as oven cavity size affect cooking performance. The vast majority of microwave ovens sold today are either 600, 650 and 700 watt ovens, but there are many ovens still in use which are between 400 and 500 watts.

Whatever the wattage of your oven, the HIGH/FULL setting will always be 100% of the oven's output. Thus your highest setting will correspond to HIGH.

However, the Medium and Low settings used in this book may not be equivalent to the Medium and Low settings marked on your oven. As these settings vary according to power input we have included the calculation (left) so you can estimate the correct setting for your oven. This simple calculation should be done before you use the recipes for the first time, to ensure successful results. Multiply the percentage power required by the total number of settings on your oven and divide by 100 to find the *correct setting*.

GENERAL RECIPE NOTES

SMALL BOWL = about 900 ml (1½ pints)
MEDIUM BOWL = about 2.3 litres (4 pints)
LARGE BOWL = about 3.4 litres (6 pints)

COVERING Cook, uncovered, unless otherwise stated. When a recipe states 'cover with cling film, pulling back one corner to let steam escape' you may cover with a lid if you prefer.

BROWNING DISHES Unless otherwise stated, 'browning dish' refers to a 25 cm (10 inch) browning dish.

EGGS Use size 3 or 4 unless otherwise stated.

IF YOUR OVEN POWER OUTPUT IS LOWER THAN 650 WATTS, THEN YOU MUST ALLOW A LONGER COOKING AND THAWING TIME FOR ALL RECIPES AND CHARTS IN THIS BOOK

ADD APPROXIMATELY 10–15 SECONDS PER MINUTE FOR A 600 WATT OVEN, AND 15–20 SECONDS PER MINUTE FOR A 500 WATT OVEN.

ALWAYS CHECK FOOD BEFORE THE END OF COOKING TIME, TO ENSURE THAT IT DOES NOT GET OVERCOOKED. DON'T FORGET TO ALLOW FOR STANDING TIME.

———IN THIS BOOK———

HIGH refers to 100%/full power output of 600–700 watts.
MEDIUM refers to 60% of full power.
LOW is 35% of full power.

BREAKFAST

POACHED FRUIT

SERVES 1

5 ml (1 level tsp) sugar, or to taste
5 ml (1 tsp) lemon juice
175 g (6 oz) prepared fruit, such as pear, apple, plum, apricot

♦ Put the sugar and 30 ml (2 tbsp) water in a medium bowl or ovenproof serving bowl and microwave on HIGH for 2 minutes. Stir until the sugar dissolves, then stir in the lemon juice.

♦ Cut the fruit into small even-sized pieces and stir into the syrup. Cover with cling film, pulling back one corner to let steam escape and microwave on HIGH for 3–6 minutes or until the fruit is tender, stirring occasionally.

♦ Leave to stand for 3 minutes. Serve hot or cold, on its own or with muesli.

TO SERVE 2

Double the ingredients, adding sugar to taste.
In Point 1: Microwave on HIGH for 3 minutes.
In Point 2: Microwave on HIGH for 4–8 minutes, or until tender.

FRUIT COMPOTE WITH YOGURT

SERVES 2

♦ Put the apricots, prunes and apple or pear into a medium ovenproof serving bowl.
♦ Pour over the orange juice and 100 ml (4 fl oz) water, then add the lemon rind. Mix together well. Cover with cling film, pulling back one corner to let steam escape, and microwave on HIGH for 8–10 minutes or until the fruits are almost tender, stirring occasionally.
♦ Leave to stand for 5 minutes, then serve warm or chilled and sprinkled with the walnuts, if liked. Serve with natural yogurt.

50 g (2 oz) dried apricots
50 g (2 oz) dried prunes
25 g (1 oz) dried apple or pear
300 ml (½ pint) fresh orange juice
strip of lemon rind
30 ml (2 level tbsp) chopped walnuts (optional)
natural yogurt, to serve

DATE AND APPLE PORRIDGE

SERVES 2

♦ Put the butter into a medium ovenproof serving bowl, stir in the bran and sugar and microwave on HIGH for 1 minute.
♦ Stir in the milk and mix together well, then sprinkle in the porridge oats.
♦ Microwave on HIGH for 4–5 minutes or until boiling, stirring every minute.
♦ Meanwhile, stone and roughly chop the dates. Roughly chop but do not peel the apple, discarding the core.
♦ Stir in the dates and apple and microwave on HIGH for 3 minutes, stirring frequently. Cook for an extra 2 minutes if a very thick consistency is preferred.
♦ Cover and leave to stand for 2–3 minutes. Serve hot.

15 g (½ oz) butter or margarine
15 ml (1 level tbsp) bran (optional)
15 ml (1 level tbsp) dark soft brown sugar
350 ml (12 fl oz) milk
40 g (1½ oz) porridge oats
50 g (2 oz) dried dates
1 eating apple

CREAMY SCRAMBLED EGG
WITH SMOKED SALMON

SERVES 1

25 g (1 oz) smoked salmon trimmings
2 eggs, size 2
30 ml (2 tbsp) double cream or milk
25 g (1 oz) butter
salt and pepper
buttered toast, to serve
chopped fresh parsley, to garnish

♦ Cut the salmon into small pieces and set aside.
♦ Put the eggs, cream and butter into a medium bowl and season with a little salt and lots of pepper. Whisk together well.
♦ Microwave on HIGH for 1 minute or until the mixture just begins to set around the edge of the bowl. Whisk vigorously to incorporate the set egg mixture.
♦ Add the smoked salmon and microwave on HIGH for 1½–2 minutes, whisking every 30 seconds and taking care not to break up the salmon, until the eggs are just set but still very soft.
♦ Check the seasoning, then spoon on to the toast. Garnish with chopped parsley and serve immediately.

TO SERVE 2

Double all the ingredients.
In Point 3: Microwave on HIGH for 2 minutes or until the mixture just begins to set around the edge.
In Point 4: Microwave on HIGH for 2 minutes or until the eggs are just set.

OEUF EN COCOTTE

SERVES 1

25 g (1 oz) button mushrooms
salt and pepper
2 drops of lemon juice
5 ml (1 level tsp) chopped fresh parsley
1.25 ml (¼ level tsp) plain flour
1 egg
15 ml (1 tbsp) double cream
chopped fresh parsley, to garnish
buttered toast, to serve

♦ Roughly chop the mushrooms and put into a 150 ml (¼ pint) ramekin dish. Microwave on HIGH for 30 seconds or until the mushrooms are almost cooked.
♦ Season with salt and pepper and stir in the lemon juice and parsley. Sprinkle in the flour and mix together well. Microwave on HIGH for 30 seconds or until slightly thickened, stirring frequently.
♦ Break the egg into the dish on top of the mushroom mixture. Gently prick the yolk with a cocktail stick or fine skewer.
♦ Microwave on MEDIUM for 1–1½ minutes or until the white is just set. Spoon over the cream and microwave on MEDIUM for 30 seconds. Leave to stand for 2 minutes. Garnish with chopped parsley and serve hot with buttered toast.

TO SERVE 2

Double the ingredients.
In Point 1: Put the mushrooms into 2 ramekins and microwave on HIGH for 1 minute or until the mushrooms are almost cooked.
In Point 2: Put 1.25 ml (¼ level tsp) plain flour into each of the ramekins and microwave on HIGH for 30–45 seconds.
In Point 4: Cook the ramekins on MEDIUM for 1½–2 minutes or until the egg whites are just set.

opposite: Creamy Scrambled Egg with Smoked Salmon (see above)

POACHED EGGS ON A MUFFIN

SERVES 2

♦ Put 30 ml (2 tbsp) water into each of two 150 ml (¼ pint) ramekin dishes. Add a large pinch of salt to each ramekin. Microwave on HIGH for 1 minute or until boiling.

♦ Break an egg into each dish and prick the yolks carefully with a cocktail stick or fine skewer.

♦ Cover loosely with cling film or a double thickness of greaseproof paper and microwave on MEDIUM for 1½–2 minutes or until the white is nearly set. Leave to stand.

♦ Cut the muffin in half and put on a serving plate. Sprinkle with the cheese and microwave on HIGH for 30 seconds or until the cheese has almost melted. Transfer one muffin half to another serving plate.

♦ Drain the eggs and spoon one egg on to each muffin half. Season with salt and pepper and serve immediately with toasted, buttered muffins.

salt and pepper
2 eggs
1 muffin
40 g (1½ oz) Cheddar cheese, grated
toasted muffins and butter, to serve

BACON AND EGG

SERVES 1

♦ Lightly oil a browning dish and preheat on HIGH for 3–4 minutes.

♦ Meanwhile, snip the bacon fat at intervals. Quickly put the bacon rashers into the browning dish, keeping them towards the edge of the dish. Press down and microwave on HIGH for 30–45 seconds.

♦ Turn the bacon over, then quickly break the egg into the centre of the dish. Prick the yolk using a cocktail stick or fine skewer and cover with a lid or cling film, pulling back one corner to allow steam to escape. Microwave on HIGH for 30–45 seconds or until the egg is nearly set.

♦ Leave to stand, covered, for 1 minute until the egg is set, then serve.

2 rashers back bacon, rinded
1 egg

TO SERVE 2

Double the ingredients.
In Point 2: Cook the bacon on HIGH for 1 minute.
In Point 3: Cook the eggs for 1–1½ minutes or until nearly set.
In Point 4: Leave to stand for 1–2 minutes or until both eggs are set.

opposite: Prawns and Lettuce Cooked in Brandy and Cream (see page 27)

FRENCH TOAST

SERVES 2

4 large slices of white bread
1 egg
75 ml (3 fl oz) milk
15 ml (1 tbsp) vegetable oil
15 g (½ oz) butter or margarine
salt and pepper or caster sugar, to serve

♦ Preheat a browning dish for 8–10 minutes.

♦ Meanwhile, cut the crusts off the bread and cut each slice in half.

♦ Beat the egg and milk together in a shallow dish. Dip the bread fingers in this mixture, making sure that each piece is completely covered.

♦ Stir the oil and butter into the browning dish, then quickly add the bread fingers. Microwave on HIGH for 1 minute, then turn the microwave on HIGH for 1–2 minutes or until the bread feels firm.

♦ Sprinkle with salt and pepper or sugar and serve hot with bacon or marmalade, if liked.

SMOKED HADDOCK KEDGEREE

SERVES 2

75 g (3 oz) long grain white rice
salt and pepper
175 g (6 oz) smoked haddock fillet
25 g (1 oz) butter or margarine, cut into pieces
1 egg, hard-boiled and chopped
30 ml (2 tbsp) chopped fresh parsley
30 ml (2 tbsp) double cream (optional)
10 ml (2 tsp) lemon juice
chopped fresh parsley, to garnish

♦ Put the rice and salt to taste in a medium bowl. Pour over 300 ml (½ pint) boiling water and cover with cling film, pulling back one corner to let steam escape. Microwave on HIGH for 10–12 minutes or until the rice is tender and the liquid has been absorbed. Set aside, covered.

♦ Put the haddock in a shallow dish with 30 ml (2 tbsp) water. Cover with cling film, pulling back one corner to let steam escape, and microwave on HIGH for 3–4 minutes or until fish is cooked.

♦ Meanwhile, stir the remaining ingredients, except the parsley, into the cooked rice, mixing together carefully with a fork. Season with salt and pepper, if necessary.

♦ Drain and flake the fish, discarding the skin. Stir into the rice mixture.

♦ Microwave on HIGH for 2–3 minutes or until heated through, stirring occasionally. Garnish with chopped fresh parsley and serve immediately.

HERRINGS IN OATMEAL

SERVES 2

♦ Preheat a browning dish for 8–10 minutes.

♦ Meanwhile, bone the herrings. With a sharp knife cut off the heads just behind the gills, then cut along the belly towards the tail so that the fish can be opened out.

♦ Place the fish flat on a board, skin side upwards and, with the heel of your hand, press along the backbone to loosen it.

♦ Turn the fish over and lift out the backbone, using the tip of a knife if necessary to help pull the bone away cleanly.

♦ Discard the bone, then wash and dry the fish. Season the inside of each herring with salt and pepper, then coat the fish in the oatmeal.

♦ Put the butter and oil in the browning dish, then quickly add the herrings. Microwave on HIGH for 1 minute, then turn them over and microwave on HIGH for 1–2 minutes, or until tender.

♦ Sprinkle over the lemon juice. Serve immediately with a little of the butter spooned over and garnished with lemon wedges and parsley.

2 small herrings, cleaned
salt and pepper
30 ml (2 level tbsp) medium oatmeal
15 g (½ oz) butter or margarine
15 ml (1 tbsp) vegetable oil
5 ml (1 tsp) lemon juice
lemon wedges and parsley, to garnish

DEVILLED KIDNEYS

SERVES 1

♦ Skin the kidneys, cut each one in half lengthways and snip out the cores with scissors.

♦ Put the butter into a medium bowl with the shallot or onion, the curry powder, mustard powder, tomato purée and cayenne pepper. Microwave on HIGH for 3–4 minutes or until the shallot is softened, stirring frequently.

♦ Stir in the kidneys, the Worcestershire sauce and 15–30 ml (1–2 tbsp) water, to make a moist consistency.

♦ Cover with cling film, pulling back one corner to let steam escape. Microwave on HIGH for 2–3 minutes or until the kidneys are just cooked, shaking the bowl occasionally. Season with salt and pepper and serve immediately.

TO SERVE 2

Double the ingredients.
In Point 2: Microwave the shallot on HIGH for 4–5 minutes or until softened.
In Point 4: Microwave on HIGH for 4–5 minutes or until the kidneys are just cooked.

2 lamb's kidneys
15 g (½ oz) butter or margarine
1 shallot or ½ small onion, skinned and finely chopped
2.5 ml (½ level tsp) curry powder
pinch of mustard powder
10 ml (2 level tsp) tomato purée
pinch of cayenne pepper
dash of Worcestershire sauce
salt and pepper

MUSHROOMS ON TOAST

SERVES 1

15 g (½ oz) butter or margarine
100 g (4 oz) button mushrooms, halved
pinch of dried thyme
2.5 ml (½ tsp) lemon juice
5 ml (1 level tsp) plain flour
5 ml (1 tsp) mushroom ketchup
salt and pepper
5 ml (1 tsp) chopped fresh parsley, to garnish
1 slice buttered toast, to serve

♦ Put the butter into a medium bowl and microwave on HIGH for 30 seconds or until melted.

♦ Stir in the mushrooms, thyme, lemon juice and 15 ml (1 tbsp) water, and microwave on HIGH for 2–3 minutes or until the mushrooms are cooked, stirring occasionally.

♦ Sprinkle in the flour and mix together well. Microwave on HIGH for 1 minute or until thickened, stirring occasionally.

♦ Stir in the mushroom ketchup and season to taste with salt and pepper. Microwave on HIGH for 2 minutes to develop the flavour.

♦ Spoon on to the toast, garnish with parsley and serve immediately.

TO SERVE 2

Double the ingredients.
In Point 1: Cook the butter on HIGH for 45 seconds or until melted.
In Point 2: Cook the mushrooms on HIGH for 3–4 minutes, or until cooked.
In Point 4: Cook on HIGH for 2–3 minutes.

POTATO PANCAKES

SERVES 2

2 large old potatoes, about 225 g (8 oz) each
1 egg, beaten
15 ml (1 level tbsp) plain flour
salt and pepper
freshly grated nutmeg
100 ml (4 fl oz) milk
15 ml (1 tbsp) vegetable oil

♦ Wash the potatoes and prick all over with a fork. Put in the oven on absorbent kitchen paper and microwave on HIGH for 12 minutes or until soft, turning over once during cooking.

♦ Preheat a browning dish for 8–10 minutes.

♦ Meanwhile, cut the potatoes in half and scoop the flesh out into a bowl. Stir in the egg and flour and season with salt, pepper and nutmeg. Mash until smooth, then beat in the milk.

♦ Put the oil in the browning dish, then quickly add the potato mixture in an even layer. Microwave on HIGH for 7 minutes or until firm. Cut into quarters and serve immediately with bacon, if liked.

APRICOT JAM

MAKES ABOUT ONE 350 g (12 oz) JAR

♦ Drain the apricots, reserving the syrup. Put into a blender or food processor with 150 ml (¼ pint) of the syrup, the lemon juice and the sugar.
♦ Blend until smooth, then pour into a large bowl. Stir in the dried apricots.
♦ Microwave on HIGH for 10–15 minutes or until thick and reduced, stirring occasionally.
♦ Meanwhile, thoroughly wash a 350 g (12 oz) jar. When the jam is cooked, pour 60 ml (4 tbsp) water into the washed jar and microwave on HIGH for 1–1½ minutes or until the water is boiling.
♦ Using oven gloves, pour out the water, invert the jar on to absorbent kitchen paper and leave to drain for a minute.
♦ Pour the jam into the hot jar. Place a disc of waxed paper across the surface and cover the jar with dampened cellophane, securing with an elastic band. Label the jar.

425 g (15 oz) can apricot halves in syrup
10 ml (2 tsp) lemon juice
75 g (3 oz) granulated sugar
25 g (1 oz) dried apricots, thinly shredded

LIME CURD

MAKES ABOUT TWO 350 g (12 oz) JARS

♦ Thoroughly wash two 350 g (12 oz) jars and pour 60 ml (4 tbsp) water into each. Set aside.
♦ Put the lime rind and juice in a medium bowl. Gradually whisk in the eggs, sugar and butter, using a balloon whisk.
♦ Microwave on HIGH for 4–6 minutes or until thickened, whisking frequently.
♦ When the curd is cooked, microwave the jam jars on HIGH for 1–1½ minutes or until the water is boiling. Using oven gloves, pour out the water and invert the jars on to absorbent kitchen paper.
♦ Meanwhile, whisk the curd frequently for 3–4 minutes or until it starts to cool and thicken further.
♦ Pour the curd into the hot sterilised jars, place a disc of waxed paper across the surface of the curd and cover the jars with dampened cellophane, securing with an elastic band. The curd will keep in a refrigerator for 3–4 weeks.

finely grated rind and juice of 4 limes
3 eggs, beaten
250 g (9 oz) caster sugar
75 g (3 oz) unsalted butter, cut into small pieces

ORANGE MARMALADE

MAKES ABOUT 450 g (1 lb)

450 g (1 lb) Seville oranges

1 lemon

450 g (1 lb) granulated sugar

knob of butter

♦ Pare the rind of the oranges and lemon, avoiding the white pith. Cut the rind into very thin strips and set aside.

♦ Finely chop the fruit flesh, pith and pips, using a food processor or sharp knife, making sure that all the pips are chopped.

♦ Put the chopped mixture into a large bowl with 450 ml (¾ pint) boiling water.

♦ Microwave on HIGH for 10–12 minutes or until the fruit has softened, stirring occasionally.

♦ Strain through a sieve, pressing the pulp to squeeze out all of the juice. Return the juice to the bowl and discard the pulp.

♦ Stir the shredded rind into the juice and microwave on HIGH for 8–10 minutes or until the rind is soft, stirring occasionally and skimming off any scum.

♦ Add the sugar and stir until dissolved. Stir in the butter.

♦ Cover with cling film, pulling back one corner to let steam escape, and microwave on HIGH for 10–15 minutes or until setting point is reached (see note at end of recipe). Leave to stand for 5–10 minutes.

♦ Thoroughly wash a 450 g (1 lb) jar. Pour 60 ml (4 tbsp) water into the clean jar and microwave on HIGH for 1–1½ minutes or until the water is boiling.

♦ Using oven gloves, pour out the water and invert the jar on to absorbent kitchen paper. Leave to drain for a minute.

♦ Stir the marmalade to distribute the peel, then pour into the hot jar. Place a disc of waxed paper across the surface and cover the jar with dampened cellophane, securing with an elastic band. Label the jar.

TO TEST FOR SETTING POINT

Put a small plate or saucer into the refrigerator before you start to make the marmalade. When you are ready to test for the setting point, put 5 ml (1 tsp) of marmalade on to the plate. Leave it to cool, then gently push your finger through it. If the surface of the marmalade wrinkles, setting point is reached. If it does not wrinkle, cook for a further minute, then test again.

BANANA AND APPLE SPREAD

MAKES ABOUT 225 g (8 oz)

♦ Cut the bananas into small pieces and put into a medium bowl. Peel, core and finely chop the apples and add to the bananas.
♦ Stir in the mixed spice, cinnamon and apple juice and stir well to mix. Cover with cling film, pulling back one corner to let steam escape, and microwave on HIGH for 10 minutes or until the apples are tender, stirring once.
♦ Purée in a blender or food processor. Leave until cold, then store, covered in the refrigerator for up to 1 week. Use to spread on toast or bread.

75 g (3 oz) dried bananas
2 large eating apples
large pinch of ground mixed spice
large pinch of ground cinnamon
100 ml (4 fl oz) unsweetened apple juice

CRUNCHY BREAKFAST GRANOLA

SERVES 2

♦ Beat the oil and honey together and stir into the dry ingredients. Mix thoroughly.
♦ Spread the mixture evenly on a microwave baking sheet, or a large flat plate, and microwave on HIGH for 4–5 minutes, or until the mixture is lightly browned, stirring every minute.
♦ Leave to cool completely, then store in an airtight container until required. Serve with milk or yogurt and fresh fruit.

30 ml (2 tbsp) vegetable oil
30 ml (2 tbsp) clear honey
75 g (3 oz) rolled oats
30 ml (2 level tbsp) wholemeal flour
30 ml (2 level tbsp) sesame seeds
30 ml (2 level tbsp) shelled sunflower seeds
30 ml (2 level tbsp) bran
30 ml (2 level tbsp) chopped blanched almonds
large pinch ground cinnamon
large pinch ground mixed spice

LIGHT MEALS
For One

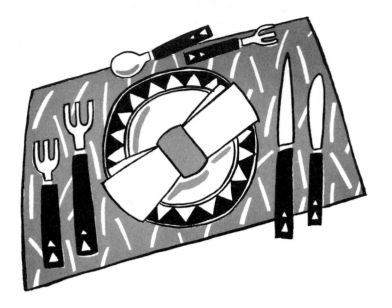

SPICY LENTIL SOUP

15 ml (1 tbsp) vegetable oil
1 shallot or ½ small onion, skinned and finely chopped
1 medium carrot, peeled and grated
1 small garlic clove, skinned and crushed
pinch of chilli powder
1.25 ml (¼ level tsp) ground cardamom
1.25 ml (¼ level tsp) ground ginger
25 g (1 oz) split red lentils
300 ml (½ pint) boiling chicken stock
75 ml (3 fl oz) milk
salt and pepper
chopped fresh coriander, to garnish

♦ Put the oil, shallot and carrot in a medium bowl and cover with cling film, pulling back one corner to let steam escape. Microwave on HIGH for 3–4 minutes, or until softened, stirring occasionally.

♦ Stir in the garlic, chilli powder, cardamom and ginger and microwave on HIGH for 1 minute, stirring once.

♦ Stir in the lentils and three quarters of the stock, cover again and microwave on HIGH for 8–10 minutes, stirring occasionally, until the lentils are cooked.

♦ Allow to cool slightly, then purée in a blender or food processor. Return to the bowl and stir in the remaining stock and the milk. Season with salt and pepper.

♦ Microwave on HIGH for 1–2 minutes, or until heated through. Garnish with coriander and serve hot.

WARM BACON AND CABBAGE
SALAD WITH MUSTARD DRESSING

◆ Put the bacon on a plate and cover loosely with absorbent kitchen paper. Microwave on HIGH for 1½–2 minutes or until the bacon is cooked. Remove the kitchen paper and cut the bacon into 2.5 cm (1 inch) pieces.
◆ Put the mustard, sugar, salt and pepper in a medium bowl and gradually blend in the oil, then the vinegar. Stir in the bacon and any accumulated cooking juices.
◆ Add the cabbage and toss together. Microwave on HIGH for 2½–3½ minutes or until the cabbage is slightly softened. Serve immediately.

4–5 rashers streaky bacon, rinded
10 ml (2 level tsp) whole grain mustard
2.5 ml (½ level tsp) granulated sugar
salt and pepper
45 ml (3 tbsp) olive or vegetable oil
5 ml (1 tsp) red wine vinegar
225 g (8 oz) green cabbage, shredded

FRENCH BEAN AND BRAZILNUT
SALAD WITH BLUE CHEESE DRESSING

◆ Top and tail the beans and cut into 4 cm (1½ inch) lengths. Put into a medium bowl with 30 ml (2 tbsp) water and cover with cling film, pulling back one corner to let steam escape. Microwave on HIGH for 4–5 minutes or until just tender. Drain and refresh in cold water.
◆ To make the dressing, put the cheese into a small bowl and mash with a fork. Stir in the mustard and salt and pepper to taste. Mix together well.
◆ Gradually beat in the oil with a fork, a little at a time, to make a thick dressing. Stir in the vinegar and the yogurt.
◆ Cut the Brazilnuts into thin slivers and put into a small bowl with the butter. Microwave on HIGH for 3–4 minutes or until browned, stirring occasionally.
◆ Arrange the radicchio or lettuce leaves on a plate. Toss the beans with the dressing and spoon over the leaves. Sprinkle with the nuts and serve immediately.

200 g (7 oz) French beans
25 g (1 oz) blue cheese, such as Stilton or Roquefort, crumbled
1.25 ml (¼ level tsp) Dijon mustard
salt and pepper
30 ml (2 tbsp) olive or vegetable oil
2.5 ml (½ tsp) white wine vinegar
15 ml (1 level tbsp) natural yogurt
15 g (½ oz) shelled Brazilnuts
15 g (½ oz) butter or margarine
radicchio or lettuce leaves, to serve

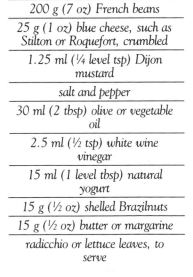

WARM BRIE WITH CELERY AND APPLE SALAD

◆

15 g (½ oz) butter or margarine
45 ml (3 level tbsp) coarse oatmeal
salt and pepper
two 25 g (1 oz) baby Brie cheeses or a 50 g (2 oz) slice of Brie
1 egg, size 6, beaten
2.5 ml (½ level tsp) Dijon mustard
15 ml (1 tbsp) chopped fresh mint
45 ml (3 tbsp) olive or vegetable oil
1.25 ml (¼ tsp) lemon juice
1 large eating apple
1 celery stick, trimmed
fresh mint, to garnish

◆ Put the butter into a small bowl and microwave on HIGH for 30 seconds or until melted. Stir in the oatmeal and microwave on HIGH for 3–4 minutes or until lightly browned, stirring occasionally.

◆ Season with salt and pepper. Brush the Brie with some of the beaten egg, then coat completely with the oatmeal. Chill for 30 minutes.

◆ Meanwhile, put the remaining egg, the mustard, mint, salt and pepper into a blender or food processor and blend together well. Slowly pour in the oil in a thin stream, with the blender still running. Blend until smooth. Add the lemon juice and blend again.

◆ Core the apple and cut the flesh into thin strips. Cut the celery into thin strips. Toss in the mint dressing and arrange on a serving plate.

◆ Put the Brie on to a small ovenproof plate, cover loosely with a piece of absorbent kitchen paper and microwave on HIGH for 15–20 seconds or until just warm. Arrange with the salad, garnish with mint and serve immediately.

CORONATION CHICKEN

◆

1 shallot or ½ small onion, skinned and finely chopped
30 ml (2 tbsp) vegetable oil
5 ml (1 level tsp) hot curry paste
5 ml (1 level tsp) tomato purée
30 ml (2 tbsp) red wine
10 ml (2 tsp) lemon juice
1 chicken quarter, about 225 g (8 oz), skinned
60 ml (4 level tbsp) mayonnaise
15 ml (1 level tbsp) apricot jam
salt and pepper
50 g (2 oz) white rice
15 ml (1 level tbsp) sultanas
25 g (1 oz) dried apricots, chopped
watercress, to garnish

◆ Put the shallot and 15 ml (1 tbsp) of the oil into a medium bowl and cover with cling film, pulling back one corner to let steam escape. Microwave on HIGH for 3–4 minutes or until softened.

◆ Stir in the curry paste, tomato purée, the red wine and half of the lemon juice. Microwave on HIGH for 5 minutes, uncovered, or until reduced by about half. Strain and leave to cool.

◆ Meanwhile, put the chicken into a roasting bag, tie loosely with a non-metallic tie and microwave on HIGH for 4–5 minutes, or until cooked. Leave to cool, then remove the meat from the bones and cut into bite-sized pieces.

◆ Beat the mayonnaise and the apricot jam into the cooled curry sauce. Season with salt and pepper. Toss the chicken pieces in the sauce. Cover and chill.

◆ Put the rice and salt to taste into a medium bowl and pour over 600 ml (1 pint) boiling water. Microwave on HIGH for 7–8 minutes or until the rice is tender.

◆ Meanwhile, make a dressing for the rice. Mix the remaining vegetable oil and lemon juice together and season with salt and pepper.

◆ Drain and rinse the rice, then stir in the dressing, sultanas and apricots while it is still hot. Leave to cool.

◆ Serve the chicken and the rice salad cold, garnished with the watercress.

PRAWNS AND LETTUCE
COOKED IN BRANDY AND CREAM

◆

◆ Peel and de-vein the prawns, leaving the tail shell intact.

◆ Put the butter into a medium bowl and microwave on HIGH for 45 seconds or until melted. Stir in the prawns and microwave on HIGH for 1½–2½ minutes, or until the prawns just turn pink, stirring frequently. Remove with a slotted spoon and set aside.

◆ Season with salt and pepper and quickly stir in the brandy and the cream. Microwave on HIGH for 4–4½ minutes or until thickened and reduced.

◆ Stir in the prawns and lettuce and mix together carefully. Microwave on HIGH for 30–45 seconds, until just heated through. Garnish with lime twists and serve immediately.

Note

If you find it difficult to buy raw prawns, buy the best quality cooked prawns in the shell and omit Points 1 and 2.

photograph opposite page 17

175 g (6 oz) medium-sized raw prawns
15 g (½ oz) butter or margarine
salt and pepper
25 ml (1½ tbsp) brandy
45 ml (3 tbsp) double cream
4 green Cos lettuce leaves, shredded
lime or lemon twists, to garnish

SOFT HERRING ROES WITH GRAPES

◆

◆ Rinse the soft roes in cold water, easing away any black threads. Dry, cut into bite-sized pieces and toss in the flour. Halve and seed the grapes.

◆ Put the butter into a medium bowl and microwave on HIGH for 30 seconds or until melted.

◆ Add the roes and any excess flour and mix together well. Microwave on HIGH for 2–2½ minutes or until the roes are almost cooked, stirring occasionally.

◆ Stir in the grapes, soured cream, lemon juice, parsley and season well with salt and pepper. Mix thoroughly and microwave on HIGH for 1–2 minutes or until hot and bubbling, stirring occasionally.

◆ Garnish with the grapes and parsley and serve immediately, with the toast.

100 g (4 oz) soft herring roes
10 ml (2 level tsp) plain flour
50 g (2 oz) green grapes
15 g (½ oz) butter or margarine
30 ml (2 level tbsp) soured cream
5 ml (1 tsp) lemon juice
15 ml (1 tbsp) chopped fresh parsley
salt and pepper
few grapes and fresh parsley, to garnish
1 slice of toast, to serve

TAGLIATELLE WITH FRESH FIGS

◆

75 g (3 oz) dried tagliatelle
salt and pepper
3 large ripe fresh figs
15 (½ oz) butter or margarine
1.25 ml (¼ level tsp) medium curry powder
30 ml (2 tbsp) soured cream
30 ml (2 level tbsp) grated Parmesan cheese
fresh herbs, to garnish (optional)

◆ Put the tagliatelle and salt to taste in a medium bowl and pour over 600 ml (1 pint) boiling water. Stir and cover with cling film, pulling back one corner to let steam escape. Microwave on HIGH for 3–4 minutes or until almost tender, stirring frequently. Leave to stand, covered (do not drain).

◆ Meanwhile, cut one of the figs in half lengthways. Reserve one of the halves to garnish, then peel and roughly chop the remainder.

◆ Put the butter, chopped figs and curry powder in a shallow dish and microwave on HIGH for 2 minutes, stirring occasionally.

◆ Drain the pasta and stir into the fig mixture with the soured cream and Parmesan cheese. Season well with salt and pepper. Carefully mix together with two forks and microwave on HIGH for 1–2 minutes or until hot.

◆ Garnish with fresh herbs, if using, and the reserved fig half and serve immediately.

photograph opposite page 32

NOODLES WITH GOAT'S CHEESE AND CHIVES

◆

100 g (4 oz) dried egg noodles
salt and pepper
15 g (½ oz) butter or margarine
30 ml (2 tbsp) double cream
40 g (1½ oz) fresh goat's cheese, crumbled
15 ml (1 tbsp) snipped fresh chives
snipped fresh chives, to garnish

◆ Put the noodles and salt to taste in a medium bowl. Pour over 600 ml (1 pint) boiling water. Stir and cover with cling film, pulling back one corner to let steam escape. Microwave on HIGH for 2–3 minutes or until almost tender. Leave to stand, covered (do not drain).

◆ Meanwhile, put the butter and cream in a medium bowl and microwave on HIGH for 1–2 minutes, or until very hot. Stir in the goat's cheese, season well with salt and pepper and mix together. Microwave on HIGH for 1 minute.

◆ Drain the noodles and stir into the cheese mixture with the chives. Carefully mix together with two forks and microwave on HIGH for 1–2 minutes or until hot. Garnish with chives and serve immediately.

TARRAGON EGG ON A PASTA NEST

◆

15 g (½ oz) butter or margarine
½ small onion, skinned and chopped
1 small garlic clove, skinned and crushed
60 ml (4 tbsp) double cream
2.5 ml (½ tsp) chopped fresh tarragon, or 1.25 ml (¼ level tsp) dried
salt and pepper
50 g (2 oz) dried green tagliatelle
1 egg
fresh tarragon, to garnish

♦ Put the butter, onion and garlic in a small bowl and cover with cling film, pulling back one corner to let steam escape. Microwave on HIGH for 3–4 minutes or until softened.

♦ Stir in the cream, tarragon and lots of salt and pepper and microwave on HIGH for 1 minute. Set aside.

♦ Put the pasta into a medium bowl with salt to taste and pour over 600 ml (1 pint) boiling water. Cover with cling film, pulling back a corner to let steam escape, and microwave on HIGH for 3–4 minutes or until almost tender. Leave to stand, covered. Do not drain.

♦ Meanwhile, put 30 ml (2 tbsp) water and a large pinch of salt into a 150 ml (¼ pint) ramekin dish. Microwave on HIGH for 1 minute or until boiling.

♦ Break the egg into the ramekin and carefully prick the yolk with a cocktail stick or fine skewer.

♦ Cover loosely with cling film or a double thickness of greaseproof paper and microwave on MEDIUM for 1–1½ minutes or until the white is almost set. Leave to stand.

♦ Meanwhile, reheat the tarragon sauce on HIGH for 1–2 minutes, or until heated through.

♦ Drain the pasta and toss with half of the sauce. Season with salt and pepper. Arrange on a large serving plate to make a 'nest' for the egg.

♦ Drain the egg and put on top of the pasta. Spoon over the remaining sauce, garnish with fresh tarragon and serve immediately.

CHICKEN LIVER PATE WITH GARLIC AND MELBA TOAST

100 g (4 oz) chicken livers
1 shallot or ½ small onion, skinned
50 g (2 oz) butter
1 garlic clove, skinned and crushed
salt and pepper
2 thin slices of white bread
1 bay leaf, to garnish

♦ Trim the chicken livers, cutting away any ducts and gristle. Cut into small pieces. Finely chop the shallot and put into a medium bowl with 25 g (1 oz) of the butter.

♦ Cover the bowl with cling film, pulling back one corner to let steam escape and microwave on HIGH for 3–4 minutes or until softened, stirring occasionally.

♦ Stir in the chicken livers and the garlic, recover and microwave on HIGH for 2–3 minutes or until the chicken livers are cooked, stirring occasionally. Season well with salt and pepper.

♦ Allow to cool slightly, then purée in a blender or food processor with half of the remaining butter.

♦ Turn into a small serving dish or 100 ml (4 fl oz) ramekin dish and chill for about 30 minutes or until firm.

♦ Put the remaining butter in a small bowl and microwave on HIGH for 30 seconds or until melted. Skim and then spoon it over the pâté. Garnish with the bay leaf and chill while making the Melba toast.

♦ To make the Melba toast, toast the bread on both sides, then using a sharp knife cut off the crusts and slice the bread in half horizontally. Scrape off any soft crumbs.

♦ Place the bread on absorbent kitchen paper and microwave on HIGH for 30–40 seconds until dry and crisp. Serve with the pâté.

CHEESE AND SALAMI PIE

◆

♦ Cut the potatoes into very thin slices, then layer in an individual round ovenproof gratin dish with the onion, Gruyère cheese and salami. Season with salt, pepper and nutmeg.

♦ Cover with cling film, pulling back one corner to let steam escape, and microwave on HIGH for 4 minutes or until the potato is almost tender.

♦ Uncover, mix the breadcrumbs and Parmesan cheese together and sprinkle evenly on the top. Microwave on HIGH for 2 minutes. Leave to stand for 5 minutes, garnish with parsley and serve with a green salad, if liked.

100 g (4 oz) potatoes, peeled
½ small onion, skinned and very thinly sliced
50 g (2 oz) Gruyère cheese, grated
25 g (1 oz) salami, rinded, thinly sliced and cut into strips
salt and pepper
freshly grated nutmeg
30 ml (2 level tbsp) fresh breadcrumbs
10 ml (2 level tsp) grated Parmesan cheese
chopped fresh parsley, to garnish

MUSHROOM SOUFFLE OMELETTE

◆

♦ Put the butter into a 18 cm (7 inch) round flameproof dish and microwave on HIGH for 30 seconds or until melted. Stir in the mushrooms and microwave on HIGH for 1–2 minutes or until softened, stirring occasionally.

♦ Whisk the egg whites until stiff. Whisk the egg yolks, parsley, salt and pepper together until mixed, then fold in the egg whites.

♦ Fold into the mushroom mixture and microwave on LOW for 4–5 minutes or until the foam looks 'set'.

♦ Place under a preheated grill for 1 minute, until browned. Run a spatula gently around the edge and underneath the omelette to loosen it, then fold it in half and serve immediately. Serve with a green salad, if liked.

15 g (½ oz) butter or margarine
50 g (2 oz) button mushrooms, sliced
2 eggs, separated
15 ml (1 tbsp) chopped fresh parsley
salt and pepper

HOT CHEESE MOUSSE
WITH GREEN PEPPERCORNS

◆

50 g (2 oz) semi-hard cheese, such as Cheshire
15 ml (1 level tbsp) fresh brown breadcrumbs
5 green peppercorns, crushed
1 egg, size 6, separated
salt
savoury biscuits and fruit, to serve

◆ Grate the cheese into a medium bowl and stir in the breadcrumbs, peppercorns, egg yolk and salt to taste.
◆ Whisk the egg white until stiff, then fold into the cheese mixture. Pour into a 150 ml (¼ pint) ramekin dish.
◆ Microwave on LOW for 5–6 minutes, or until the mixture is risen and set, turning the dish once during cooking. Serve at once with biscuits and fruit.

TUNA FISHCAKES

◆

1 medium potato, about 100 g (4 oz)
knob of butter or margarine
99 g (3½ oz) can tuna in brine
5 ml (1 tsp) lemon juice
salt and pepper
15 ml (1 tbsp) chopped fresh parsley
15 ml (1 tbsp) natural yogurt
15 ml (1 level tbsp) seasoned flour
15 ml (1 tbsp) vegetable oil

◆ Prick the potato all over with a fork. Place on absorbent kitchen paper and microwave on HIGH for 4–5 minutes or until soft, turning over halfway through cooking.
◆ Preheat a browning dish for 8–10 minutes.
◆ Meanwhile, cut the potato in half, scoop out the flesh and mash with the butter. Drain the tuna and mix with the potato, lemon juice, salt and pepper and parsley. Bind together with the natural yogurt.
◆ Shape into two fish cakes about 1 cm (½ inch) thick. Coat with the seasoned flour.
◆ Add the oil to the browning dish, then quickly add the fish cakes and microwave on HIGH for 2 minutes. Turn over and microwave on HIGH for 1–2 minutes or until lightly browned. Serve immediately with a mixed salad.

opposite: Tagliatelle with Fresh Figs (see page 28)

VEGETARIAN WHOLEMEAL PIZZA

◆

♦ Put the tomatoes, garlic, onion, green pepper, tomato purée, sugar, salt and pepper in a medium bowl. Microwave on HIGH for 5–7 minutes or until the onion and pepper are softened and the liquid slightly reduced, stirring occasionally. Set aside.

♦ Preheat a browning dish on HIGH for 8–10 minutes.

♦ Meanwhile, put the flour and a pinch of salt into a bowl, then rub in the butter until the mixture resembles fine breadcrumbs. Add the milk and mix to a soft dough.

♦ Turn the dough out on to a lightly floured work surface and knead until smooth. Roll out to a 20.5 cm (8 inch) circle. Brush generously with some of the oil.

♦ Quickly put the pizza dough into the browning dish, oiled side down, and microwave on HIGH for 2–3 minutes or until the surface of the dough looks slightly dry.

♦ Brush with more oil and turn over. Microwave on HIGH for 1–2 minutes.

♦ Spread the tomato mixture evenly over the pizza base, right to the edges. Arrange the slices of Mozzarella on top.

♦ Arrange the mushrooms and olives over the top of the cheese and sprinkle with the oregano, salt and pepper to taste and any remaining oil.

♦ Microwave on HIGH for 3–4 minutes or until the cheese has melted and the mushrooms cooked. Serve immediately.

226 g (8 oz) can tomatoes, drained and chopped
1 small garlic clove, skinned and crushed
½ small onion, skinned and finely chopped
½ green pepper, seeded and chopped
5 ml (1 level tsp) tomato purée
pinch of sugar
salt and pepper
100 g (4 oz) wholemeal self raising flour
25 g (1 oz) butter or margarine
50–75 ml (2–3 fl oz) milk
25 ml (1½ tbsp) vegetable oil
50 g (2 oz) Mozzarella cheese, thinly sliced
25 g (1 oz) button mushrooms, thinly sliced
6 black olives, stoned and halved
5 ml (1 tsp) chopped fresh oregano, or 2.5 ml (½ level tsp) dried

opposite: Hot Baguette Sandwich with Salami and Red Pepper Sauce (see page 37)

S N A C K S

PIPERADE

SERVES 1

2 ripe tomatoes
15 g (½ oz) butter or margarine
½ small green pepper, seeded and chopped
½ garlic clove, skinned and crushed
1 shallot or ½ small onion, skinned and finely chopped
salt and pepper
2 eggs, beaten
French bread, to serve

◆ Prick the tomatoes with a fork and microwave on HIGH for 1 minute or until the skins burst. Peel off the skin, discard the seeds and roughly chop the flesh.

◆ Put the butter in a medium bowl and microwave on HIGH for 30 seconds or until melted. Stir in the pepper, garlic and shallot.

◆ Cover with cling film, pulling back one corner to let steam escape, and microwave on HIGH for 2½–3 minutes or until softened.

◆ Season with salt and pepper and stir in the tomatoes. Microwave on HIGH for 1 minute, then stir in the egg.

◆ Microwave on HIGH for 1–2 minutes or until the eggs are lightly scrambled, stirring frequently. Serve immediately with French bread.

TO SERVE 2

Double the ingredients.
In Point 1: Microwave on HIGH for 1½ minutes or until the skins burst.
In Point 2: Microwave on HIGH for 45 seconds or until melted.
In Point 3: Microwave on HIGH for 3–4 minutes or until softened.
In Point 5: Microwave on HIGH for 2–3 minutes or until the eggs are lightly scrambled.

MELTED CHEESE
AND HAM SANDWICH

SERVES 1

♦ Preheat a browning dish on HIGH for 4–5 minutes.
♦ Meanwhile, spread the bread slices with the mustard. Cut the cheese into thin slivers and pile on top of one slice. Cut the ham into strips and arrange evenly on top of the cheese. Season with salt and pepper.
♦ Put the second slice of bread on top, mustard side down, and spread with half of the butter. Turn the sandwich over and spread with the remaining butter.
♦ Quickly put the sandwich into the browning dish and microwave on HIGH for 30 seconds, then turn over and microwave on HIGH for 20–30 seconds or until the cheese melts. Serve immediately with a green salad.

TO SERVE 2

Reheat the browning dish for 2 minutes and repeat the recipe.

2 large slices of bread
5 ml (1 level tsp) whole grain mustard
40 g (1½ oz) Gruyère cheese
50 g (2 oz) York ham
salt and pepper
15 g (½ oz) butter or margarine
mixed green salad, to serve

GRANARY LEEK TOASTS

SERVES 2

♦ Put the butter into a medium bowl and microwave on HIGH for 45 seconds or until melted.
♦ Finely chop the leeks and stir into the melted butter. Cover with cling film, pulling back one corner to let steam escape, and microwave on HIGH for 7–8 minutes or until the leeks are very soft, stirring occasionally. Season with salt and pepper.
♦ Stir in the flour and microwave on HIGH for 2 minutes, stirring frequently.
♦ Gradually stir in the cheese and lemon juice and beat together well. Stir in the egg yolk. Microwave on HIGH for 1–2 minutes or until warmed through and slightly thickened.
♦ Cut the toast in half diagonally and arrange on 2 serving plates. Spoon on the leek mixture, garnish with parsley and serve immediately.

25 g (1 oz) butter or margarine
4 medium leeks, trimmed and washed
salt and pepper
10 ml (2 level tsp) plain flour
65 g (2½ oz) full fat soft cheese with garlic and herbs
5 ml (1 tsp) lemon juice
1 egg yolk
3 slices of granary bread, toasted
chopped fresh parsley, to garnish

CHICK-PEAS WITH
TOMATOES AND CHILLI

SERVES 2

4–6 poppadums
30 ml (2 tbsp) vegetable oil, plus extra for brushing
1 medium onion, skinned and chopped
1 garlic clove, skinned and crushed
1 green chilli, seeded and finely chopped
1.25 ml (¼ level tsp) mild chilli powder
2.5 ml (½ level tsp) ground turmeric
2.5 ml (½ level tsp) paprika
5 ml (1 level tsp) ground cumin
5 ml (1 level tsp) ground coriander
3 tomatoes, roughly chopped
425 g (15 oz) can chick-peas, drained
15 ml (1 tbsp) chopped fresh coriander
salt and pepper
fresh coriander, to garnish

♦ Brush one side of each poppadum lightly with oil. Stand, one at a time, oiled side up on absorbent kitchen paper in the microwave and cook on HIGH for 45 seconds–1 minute, until puffed all over. Set aside.

♦ Put the oil, onion, and garlic in a medium bowl and cover with cling film, pulling back one corner to let steam escape. Microwave on HIGH for 5–7 minutes or until softened.

♦ Stir in the chilli, chilli powder, turmeric, paprika, cumin and ground coriander and microwave on HIGH for 1 minute, stirring once.

♦ Stir in the tomatoes and microwave on HIGH for 3–5 minutes, or until the tomatoes reduce to a thick purée, stirring occasionally.

♦ Stir in the chick-peas, coriander, salt and pepper. Re-cover and microwave on HIGH for 2–3 minutes, or until heated through, stirring occasionally.

♦ Garnish with coriander and serve with the poppadums.

HOT BAGUETTE SANDWICH WITH SALAMI AND RED PEPPER SAUCE

SERVES 2

◆ Put the oil, onion, paprika, sugar, cayenne pepper and chopped red pepper in a medium bowl. Cover with cling film, pulling back one corner to let steam escape, and microwave on HIGH for 5–7 minutes or until softened, stirring occasionally.

◆ Stir in the flour and microwave on HIGH for 30 seconds.

◆ Gradually stir in the chicken stock and microwave on HIGH for 5–6 minutes stirring frequently, until the pepper is soft and the sauce has thickened.

◆ Meanwhile, cut the Mozzarella into thin slices and remove the rind from the salami. Cut the baguette in half widthways, then cut each half in half lengthways. Arrange a layer of Mozzarella on two halves. Top with a layer of salami. Season with pepper.

◆ When the sauce is cooked, let it cool a little then purée in a blender or food processor until smooth. Spoon on top of the salami. Top with a few olives, if using. Put the other half of the baguette on top of each half to make two sandwiches.

◆ Wrap each sandwich in greaseproof paper and microwave on HIGH for 1–1½ minutes or until the sandwiches are just warmed through. Serve immediately.

photograph opposite page 33

15 ml (1 tbsp) olive or vegetable oil
1 small onion, skinned and chopped
5 ml (1 level tsp) paprika
2.5 ml (½ level tsp) sugar
pinch of cayenne pepper
1 small red pepper, cored, seeded and chopped
15 ml (1 level tbsp) plain flour
150 ml (¼ pint) chicken stock
225 g (8 oz) Mozzarella cheese
4 thin slices of Danish salami
1 small baguette, about 30.5 cm (12 inches) long
salt and pepper
few black olives, stoned (optional)

HOT AVOCADO AND PRAWNS

SERVES 2

◆ Put the shallot and oil in a medium bowl and cover with cling film, pulling back one corner to let steam escape. Microwave on HIGH for 3–4 minutes or until soft, stirring occasionally.

◆ Meanwhile, halve and stone the avocado. Using a teaspoon, scoop out most of the flesh into a bowl, leaving a 1 cm (½ inch) shell. Rub the inside of the avocado shell with half of the lime juice.

◆ Mash the scooped-out avocado with a fork to a smooth pulp. Gradually mix in the yogurt, mayonnaise, mustard and remaining lime juice. Season well with salt and pepper.

◆ Stir the prawns into the cooked shallot and microwave on HIGH for 1 minute, stirring occasionally.

◆ Strain the prawns, stir into the avocado and yogurt mixture, and mix together well.

◆ Microwave on HIGH for 1–2 minutes or until just heated through, stirring occasionally. Stir in the chives.

◆ Put the avocado shells on to a small ovenproof serving plate and fill with the prawn mixture. Microwave on HIGH for a further 1–2 minutes or until warmed through. Transfer one of the avocados to a second serving plate.

◆ Garnish with the lime and prawns and serve immediately.

1 shallot or ½ small onion, skinned and finely chopped
15 ml (1 tbsp) vegetable oil
1 ripe avocado
10 ml (2 tsp) lime or lemon juice
30 ml (2 level tbsp) natural yogurt
30 ml (2 level tbsp) mayonnaise
1.25 ml (¼ level tsp) prepared mustard
salt and pepper
75 g (3 oz) peeled prawns
15 ml (1 tbsp) snipped fresh chives
lime or lemon twists and unpeeled prawns, to garnish

LENTIL, MINT AND YOGURT SALAD

SERVES 2

100 g (4 oz) green lentils, washed
bouquet garni
60 ml (4 tbsp) olive or vegetable oil
30 ml (2 tbsp) lemon juice
large pinch of ground allspice
salt and pepper
45 ml (3 tbsp) chopped fresh mint
3 spring onions
3 large tomatoes
30 ml (2 tbsp) Greek strained yogurt
lemon wedges and mint sprigs, to garnish

◆ Put the lentils into a large bowl and pour over 900 ml (1½ pints) boiling water. Add the bouquet garni and cover with cling film, pulling back one corner to let steam escape. Microwave on HIGH for 10–12 minutes or until the lentils are just tender.

◆ Meanwhile, mix together the olive oil and lemon juice and season with allspice, salt and pepper. Stir in the mint.

◆ Drain the lentils and stir in the dressing. Chill for about 30 minutes.

◆ Meanwhile, trim and chop the onions and cut the tomatoes into small wedges.

◆ Stir into the lentils and mix together well. Stir in the yogurt. Season if necessary. Serve chilled, garnished with lemon wedges and mint sprigs.

photograph opposite page 48

PARMESAN MUSHROOMS

SERVES 1

25 g (1 oz) butter or margarine
4 medium flat mushrooms
1 small garlic clove, skinned and crushed
40 g (1½ oz) fresh brown breadcrumbs
75 ml (5 level tbsp) grated Parmesan cheese
10 ml (2 tsp) lemon juice
salt and pepper
grated nutmeg
15 ml (1 tbsp) chopped fresh parsley
lemon twists and fresh parsley, to garnish
French bread, to serve

◆ Put half of the butter in a small bowl and microwave on HIGH for 30 seconds or until melted.

◆ Finely chop the mushroom stalks and one of the mushrooms and stir into the melted butter with the garlic. Microwave on HIGH for 45 seconds or until softened, stirring once.

◆ Stir in the breadcrumbs, half of the Parmesan and the lemon juice. Mix together well and season with salt, pepper and nutmeg. Stir in half of the parsley.

◆ Arrange the mushroom caps on an ovenproof serving plate and spoon on the stuffing mixture.

◆ Sprinkle with the remaining Parmesan and parsley and dot with the remaining butter.

◆ Microwave on HIGH for 2–3 minutes or until the mushrooms are cooked. Garnish with lemon twists and parsley and serve with French bread.

TO SERVE 2

Double all the ingredients except the garlic.
In Point 1: Microwave on HIGH for 45 seconds or until melted.
In Point 2: Microwave on HIGH for 1½ minutes or until softened.
In Point 6: Microwave on HIGH for 3–5 minutes or until the mushrooms are cooked.

AUBERGINE PUREE WITH
RED PEPPER AND PITTA BREAD

SERVES 2

♦ Wash the aubergine and prick all over with a fork.
♦ Microwave on HIGH for 4–5 minutes or until very soft when pressed with a finger. Leave to stand.
♦ Meanwhile, put the oil in a medium bowl, with the chilli powder, cumin, coriander and garlic. Microwave on HIGH for 2 minutes, stirring occasionally. Stir in the lemon juice.
♦ Cut the aubergine in half and scoop out the flesh. Mix with the cooked spices, mashing with a fork to make a pulp.
♦ Season well with salt and pepper and gradually beat in the yogurt. Stir in the chopped parsley.
♦ Cut the pepper into neat thin strips and arrange on a serving plate.
♦ Spoon the aubergine purée into two individual serving bowls and garnish with the black olives and parsley.
♦ Microwave the pitta bread on HIGH for 30 seconds or until warm. Cut into fingers and arrange on the serving plate with the pepper.
♦ Serve immediately with the aubergine purée.

1 small aubergine
15 ml (1 tbsp) olive or vegetable oil
pinch of mild chilli powder
2.5 ml (½ level tsp) ground cumin
2.5 ml (½ level tsp) ground coriander
½ small garlic clove, skinned and crushed
10 ml (2 tsp) lemon juice
salt and pepper
150 ml (¼ pint) natural yogurt
15 ml (1 tbsp) chopped fresh parsley
1 red pepper, cored and seeded
black olives and chopped fresh parsley, to garnish
2 pitta breads, to serve

BAKED POTATO WITH
CHEESE AND FRESH HERBS

SERVES 1

♦ Wash the potato and prick all over with a fork. Place on absorbent kitchen paper and microwave on HIGH for 6–8 minutes or until soft, turning over once during cooking.
♦ Cut a large deep cross in the top of the potato and scoop out the flesh with a teaspoon into a bowl, taking care not to puncture the skin and leaving a thin shell.
♦ Mash the scooped-out flesh with the butter, half of the cheese, the cream and 15 ml (1 tbsp) of the herbs. Season well with salt, pepper and nutmeg.
♦ Pile the mixture back into the potato shell, put on an ovenproof serving plate and microwave on HIGH for 1–2 minutes or until heated through.
♦ Sprinkle with the remaining cheese and herbs. Microwave on HIGH for 30 seconds or until the cheese is just melted. Serve immediately with a tomato salad.

one 200 g (7 oz) old potato
15 g (½ oz) butter or margarine
50 g (2 oz) Cheddar cheese, grated
30 ml (2 tbsp) double cream or milk
25 ml (1½ tbsp) chopped fresh mixed herbs
salt and pepper
freshly grated nutmeg
tomato salad, to serve

TO SERVE 2

Double the ingredients.
In Point 1: Microwave on HIGH for 8–10 minutes or until soft.
In Point 4: Microwave on HIGH for 2–3 minutes or until heated through.
In Point 5: Microwave on HIGH for 45 seconds or until the cheese is melted.

KIDNEYS CURRIED IN PITTA BREAD

SERVES 1

3 lamb's kidneys
15 ml (1 tbsp) vegetable oil
1 small onion, skinned and finely sliced
2.5 ml (½ level tsp) curry powder
2.5 ml (½ level tsp) ground cumin
2.5 ml (½ level tsp) ground turmeric
5 ml (1 tsp) lemon juice
75 ml (3 fl oz) chicken stock
5 ml (1 level tsp) tomato purée
salt and pepper
1 pitta bread
15 ml (1 level tbsp) mango chutney
1 small carrot, peeled and coarsely grated
few lettuce leaves, shredded

♦ Skin the kidneys and cut into small pieces, discarding the cores.

♦ Put the oil and half of the sliced onion into a small bowl. Cover with cling film, pulling back one corner to let steam escape, and microwave on HIGH for 2–3 minutes or until softened.

♦ Stir in the curry powder, ground cumin and turmeric. Microwave on HIGH for 1 minute.

♦ Stir in the kidneys and microwave on HIGH for 1–2 minutes or until just changing colour, stirring occasionally.

♦ Stir in the lemon juice, stock, tomato purée, salt and pepper. Re-cover and microwave on HIGH for 2–3 minutes or until the kidneys are cooked.

♦ Microwave the pitta bread on HIGH for 15 seconds or until warm. Cut in half widthways and split open to make two 'pockets'. Spread with mango chutney.

♦ Mix the remaining onion with the carrot and lettuce and use to fill the pitta bread. Spoon the kidney mixture on top of the salad and serve immediately.

TO SERVE 2

Double the ingredients.

In Point 2: Cook the onion on HIGH for 3–5 minutes or until softened.

In Point 4: Cook the kidneys on HIGH for 3–5 minutes or until just changing colour.

In Point 5: Microwave on HIGH for 4–5 minutes or until the kidneys are cooked.

LEMON AND HERB BREAD

SERVES 2

♦ Slice the bread at 2.5 cm (1 inch) intervals almost through to the base.
♦ Put the butter into a small bowl and microwave on HIGH for 10–15 seconds or until just soft enough to beat.
♦ Stir in the grated lemon rind and 5 ml (1 tsp) of the lemon juice. Stir in the remaining ingredients and mix together well.
♦ Spread each side of the bread slices with the lemon and herb butter. Press the loaf together to reshape.
♦ Wrap in greaseproof paper and microwave on HIGH for 1 minute or until the bread is just warmed through. Serve immediately as a snack or as an accompaniment.

1 small French loaf, about 30.5 cm (12 inches) long
50 g (2 oz) butter or margarine
finely grated rind and juice of ½ lemon
25 ml (1½ tbsp) chopped fresh mixed herbs
2.5 ml (½ level tsp) Dijon mustard
salt and pepper

GRUYERE AND CARAWAY BREAD

SERVES 2

♦ Slice the rolls at 2.5 cm (1 inch) intervals, almost through to the base.
♦ Put the butter into a small bowl and microwave on HIGH for 10–15 seconds or until just soft enough to beat.
♦ Stir in half of the Gruyère cheese, the Parmesan, caraway seeds and salt and pepper to taste. Mix together.
♦ Spread both sides of the slices with the butter mixture. Press the slices together to reshape the rolls and sprinkle with the remaining Gruyère.
♦ Wrap each roll in greaseproof paper and microwave on HIGH for 1 minute or until the bread is just warmed through. Serve immediately as a snack or an accompaniment.

2 long crusty wholemeal rolls, about 15 cm (6 inches) long
40 g (1½ oz) butter or margarine
75 g (3 oz) Gruyère cheese, grated
15 ml (1 level tbsp) grated Parmesan cheese
5 ml (1 level tsp) caraway seeds
salt and pepper

PEPPERONI AND BAKED BEAN SNACK

SERVES 2

1 small onion, skinned and finely chopped
10 ml (2 tsp) vegetable oil
large pinch chilli powder
2.5 ml (½ level tsp) curry powder
2.5 ml (½ level tsp) dark brown sugar
5 ml (1 tsp) Worcestershire sauce
2.5 ml (½ tsp) mild mustard
10 ml (2 tsp) tomato purée
450 g (15.9 oz) can baked beans
75 g (3 oz) thickly sliced pepperoni
3 thick slices toast

♦ Put the onion, vegetable oil, chilli powder and curry powder in a medium bowl. Cover with cling film, pulling back one corner to let steam escape, and microwave on HIGH for 3–4 minutes or until the onion is softened, stirring once.

♦ Stir in the sugar, Worcestershire sauce, mustard, tomato purée and baked beans and microwave on HIGH for 2 minutes until hot, stirring once.

♦ Remove the rind from the pepperoni and cut each slice in half. Stir into the bean mixture and microwave on HIGH for 1–2 minutes until heated through.

♦ Arrange the toast on two serving plates, pour over the pepperoni and bean mixture and serve immediately.

PRAWN AND SESAME PARCELS WITH BEANSPROUT SALAD

SERVES 2

15 ml (1 tbsp) vegetable oil
50 g (2 oz) button mushrooms, chopped
1 cm (½ inch) piece of fresh root ginger, peeled and grated
2 spring onions, trimmed and finely chopped
75 g (3 oz) peeled prawns
20 ml (4 tsp) soy sauce
100 g (4 oz) strong plain wholemeal flour
salt and pepper
15 ml (1 level tbsp) sesame seeds
1 egg yolk
25 g (1 oz) beansprouts
1.25 ml (¼ level tsp) Chinese 5-spice powder

♦ Put the oil, mushrooms, ginger, spring onions, prawns and half of the soy sauce into a medium bowl, and microwave on HIGH for 2 minutes or until the mushrooms are softened.

♦ Put the flour, salt and pepper to taste with the sesame seeds in a medium bowl. Make a well in the centre. Add the egg yolk and about 30 ml (2 tbsp) cold water to make a soft dough.

♦ Knead the dough lightly then roll out on a lightly floured surface to a 30.5 cm (12 inch) square. Cut into four squares, then divide the filling between them.

♦ Brush the edges of the pastry with water, then bring the four points of each square together and seal to form an envelope-shaped parcel.

♦ Put the parcels on to two small ovenproof serving plates. Divide the beansprouts between the two plates. Mix the remaining soy sauce with the 5-spice powder and drizzle over the beansprouts.

♦ Cover each plate loosely with cling film and microwave on HIGH for 4–5 minutes or until the parcels are just set and firm to the touch. Serve immediately.

CHICKEN TACOS

SERVES 2

♦ Roughly chop one of the tomatoes and put into a medium bowl with the oil, onion, chicken and tomato purée. Cover with cling film, pulling back one corner to let steam escape, and microwave on HIGH for 5 minutes or until the chicken is tender, stirring occasionally. Season to taste with Tabasco sauce and salt and pepper.

♦ Divide the filling between the taco shells and pile the shredded lettuce on top. Sprinkle with the grated cheese and serve immediately.

2 large tomatoes
15 ml (1 tbsp) vegetable oil
1 small onion, skinned and chopped
1 chicken breast fillet, skinned and diced
15 ml (1 tbsp) tomato purée
few drops of Tabasco sauce
salt and pepper
4 Mexican taco shells
shredded lettuce
50 g (2 oz) Cheddar cheese, grated

CLUB SANDWICH

SERVES 1

♦ Arrange the bacon in a single layer on a large flat plate. Cover with a double layer of absorbent kitchen paper and microwave on HIGH for 3–3½ minutes or until the bacon is cooked. Quickly remove the kitchen paper and leave the bacon to stand for 2 minutes or until slightly crisp.

♦ Meanwhile, spread one side of each slice of toast with the mayonnaise and season with pepper and a little salt.

♦ To assemble the sandwich, arrange two slices of bacon on top of one slice of toast, top with a few lettuce leaves, one slice of turkey and half of the sliced tomato. Press another slice of toast on top, mayonnaise side down, and repeat with the remaining ingredients.

♦ Cut the sandwich diagonally into quarters and secure each one with a cocktail stick. Arrange with crust sides down on a serving plate and serve at once.

4 rashers streaky bacon, rinded
3 large slices bread, toasted
30 ml (2 tbsp) mayonnaise
salt and pepper
few lettuce leaves
2 slices cooked turkey or chicken
1 tomato, sliced

TO SERVE 2

Double the ingredients.
In Point 1: Microwave on HIGH for 5–6 minutes or until the bacon is cooked.

L U N C H

CHILLED BUTTERMILK AND DILL SOUP

SERVES 1

1 small leek, white part only
15 g (½ oz) butter or margarine
1 medium potato, weighing about 100 g (4 oz), peeled
150 ml (¼ pint) hot chicken stock
15 ml (1 tbsp) chopped fresh dill
salt and pepper
150 ml (¼ pint) buttermilk

♦ Chop the leek very finely, wash and drain well. Put into a medium bowl with the butter. Grate in the potato.

♦ Cover with cling film, pulling back one corner to let steam escape, and microwave on HIGH for 3–4 minutes or until the vegetables have softened, stirring occasionally.

♦ Stir in the chicken stock and half of the dill. Re-cover and microwave on HIGH for 5–8 minutes or until the potato is very soft. Season well with salt and pepper.

♦ Allow to cool a little, then purée in a blender or food processor. Stir in the buttermilk and pour into a serving bowl. Chill for at least 2 hours before serving.

♦ To serve, sprinkle the remaining chopped dill on top. Serve with wholemeal bread, if liked.

TO SERVE 2

Double all the ingredients.

In Point 2: Microwave on HIGH for 4–5 minutes or until softened, stirring occasionally.

In Point 3: Microwave on HIGH for 10–12 minutes or until the potato is soft.

SMOKED HADDOCK CHOWDER

SERVES 2

♦ Put the haddock and 15 ml (1 tbsp) of the milk in a shallow dish. Cover with cling film, pulling back one corner to allow steam to escape, and microwave on HIGH for 2–3 minutes or until tender. Set aside.

♦ Put the bacon, oil, onion, potato and celery in a medium bowl and microwave on HIGH for 2 minutes, stirring occasionally.

♦ Sprinkle in the flour and microwave on HIGH for 30 seconds, then gradually stir in the remaining milk. Microwave on HIGH for 3–4 minutes or until boiling, then stir in the bay leaf and thyme.

♦ Cover with cling film, pulling back one corner to let steam escape, and microwave on HIGH for 10 minutes, stirring occasionally.

♦ Meanwhile, flake the haddock, discarding any bones.

♦ Stir the haddock and any cooking liquid into the soup with the parsley, salt and pepper. Cover again and microwave on HIGH for 2–3 minutes or until heated through, stirring occasionally.

♦ Leave to stand for 5 minutes, then serve with French bread, if liked.

225 g (8 oz) smoked haddock fillet, skinned
450 ml (¾ pint) milk
1 rasher streaky bacon, rinded and chopped
15 ml (1 tbsp) vegetable oil
1 small onion, skinned and thinly sliced
1 medium potato, peeled and finely diced
1 celery stick, chopped
15 ml (1 level tbsp) plain flour
1 bay leaf
pinch of dried thyme
15 ml (1 tbsp) chopped fresh parsley
salt and pepper

PEPPER AND GINGER SOUP WITH SESAME BREAD

SERVES 2

♦ Put 15 g (½ oz) of the butter into a medium bowl with the chopped pepper, onion and ginger. Cover with cling film, pulling back one corner to let steam escape, and microwave on HIGH for 7–8 minutes until the vegetables have softened, stirring occasionally.

♦ Stir in 2.5 ml (½ level tsp) of the paprika and microwave on HIGH for 1 minute, uncovered.

♦ Stir in the sugar, chicken stock, salt and pepper. Re-cover and microwave on HIGH for 5–6 minutes or until the pepper is soft.

♦ Allow to cool a little, then purée in a blender or food processor with the yogurt and pour into two serving bowls.

♦ Put the remaining butter in a small bowl and microwave on HIGH for 10–15 seconds or until just soft enough to beat. Beat in the remaining paprika, the sesame seeds and salt and pepper to taste.

♦ Cut each slice of bread into four triangles and spread the sesame butter on both sides.

♦ Arrange the bread in a circle on a sheet of greaseproof paper and microwave on HIGH for 1 minute. Turn the bread over and microwave on HIGH for a further 1 minute or until the bread is firm. Leave to stand for 2 minutes.

♦ Meanwhile, microwave the soup on LOW for 2–3 minutes or until warmed through. Garnish the soup with thin slices of red pepper and serve with the sesame bread.

40 g (1½ oz) butter or margarine
1 large red pepper, seeded and roughly chopped
1 small onion, skinned and finely chopped
1 cm (½ inch) piece of fresh ginger, peeled and grated
7.5 ml (1½ level tsp) paprika
pinch of sugar
300 ml (½ pint) chicken stock
salt and pepper
150 ml (¼ pint) natural yogurt
15 ml (1 level tbsp) sesame seeds
3 slices of bread, crusts removed
thin slices of red pepper, to garnish (optional)

CHILLED COURGETTE MOUSSE
WITH SAFFRON SAUCE

SERVES 2

275 g (10 oz) small courgettes, trimmed
15 g (½ oz) butter or margarine
7.5 ml (1½ tsp) lemon juice
100 g (4 oz) low fat soft cheese
salt and pepper
5 ml (1 level tsp) gelatine
45 ml (3 tbsp) natural yogurt
pinch of saffron strands
1 egg yolk
fresh herb sprigs, to garnish

♦ Cut one of the courgettes into very thin slices lengthways, using a potato peeler or sharp knife. Put the slices into a medium bowl with 30 ml (2 tbsp) water.

♦ Cover with cling film, pulling back one corner to let steam escape, and microwave on HIGH for 2–3 minutes or until the slices are just tender, stirring once. Drain and dry with absorbent kitchen paper.

♦ Use the courgette slices to line two oiled 150 ml (¼ pint) ramekin dishes. Set aside while making the filling.

♦ Finely chop the remaining courgettes and put into a medium bowl with half of the butter and the lemon juice.

♦ Cover with cling film, pulling back one corner to let steam escape, and microwave on HIGH for 5–6 minutes or until tender, stirring occasionally.

♦ Allow to cool slightly, then purée in a blender or food processor with the remaining butter and the cheese. Season well with salt and pepper.

♦ Put the gelatine and 15 ml (1 tbsp) water into a small bowl or cup and microwave on LOW for 1–1½ minutes or until the gelatine has dissolved, stirring occasionally. Add to the courgette purée and mix together thoroughly.

♦ Pour into the lined dishes and leave to cool. Chill for at least 1 hour or until set.

♦ Meanwhile, make the sauce. Put the yogurt, saffron, egg yolk, salt and pepper into a small bowl and microwave on LOW for 1–1½ minutes, or until slightly thickened, stirring frequently. Strain, then leave to cool.

♦ To serve, loosen the courgette moulds with a palette knife, then turn out on to two individual serving plates. Pour over the sauce, garnish with a herb sprig and serve immediately.

photograph opposite page 49

HOT MUSHROOM MOUSSE WITH HOLLANDAISE SAUCE

SERVES 2

◆ Line the base of an 11×7.5 cm (4½×3 inch) 350 ml (12 fl oz) dish with greaseproof paper.

◆ Put the butter in a large bowl and microwave on HIGH for 45 seconds or until melted.

◆ Add the mushrooms, onion and coriander, cover the dish with cling film, pulling back one corner to let the steam escape, and microwave on HIGH for 5 minutes or until softened, stirring occasionally. Leave to cool for 15 minutes.

◆ Add the cheese, 2 egg yolks and salt and pepper to taste. Turn the mixture into a blender or food processor and mix to form a purée. Return the mixture to the bowl.

◆ Whisk the egg whites until stiff, then fold into the mushroom mixture. Pour into the lined dish.

◆ Microwave on HIGH for 10 minutes or until cooked, giving the dish a quarter turn three times during cooking.

◆ Meanwhile, make the Hollandaise Sauce. Put the remaining egg yolk, lemon juice, salt and pepper into a small bowl and whisk until frothy. Cut the unsalted butter into small pieces and put in a medium bowl. Microwave on HIGH for 1½–2 minutes until melted. Add to the egg yolk mixture very slowly in a thin steady stream, whisking vigorously until the mixture is smooth and creamy. Whisk in 10 ml (2 tsp) boiling water.

◆ Microwave on LOW for 1–2 minutes or until warm and slightly thickened, whisking every 30 seconds.

◆ Lift the mushrooms out of the dish and cut in slices widthways. Arrange on two warmed serving plates and coat with the Hollandaise Sauce. Garnish with cayenne and coriander and serve warm.

25 g (1 oz) butter or margarine, cut into pieces
225 g (8 oz) mushrooms, finely chopped
½ small onion, skinned and very finely chopped
5 ml (1 level tsp) ground coriander
100 g (4 oz) curd cheese
2 eggs, separated, plus 1 egg yolk
salt and pepper
5 ml (1 tsp) lemon juice
75 g (3 oz) unsalted butter
pinch of cayenne and fresh coriander, to garnish

SPICY NUT BURGERS
WITH CORIANDER RAITA

SERVES 2

45 ml (3 tbsp) vegetable oil
1 small onion, skinned and chopped
1 medium carrot, peeled and finely grated
1 garlic clove, skinned and crushed
1 cm (½ inch) piece fresh ginger, peeled and chopped
2.5 ml (½ level tsp) coriander seeds, finely crushed
2.5 ml (½ level tsp) cumin seeds
100 g (4 oz) mixed nuts, finely chopped
25 g (1 oz) Cheddar cheese, finely grated
50 g (2 oz) brown breadcrumbs
salt and pepper
1 egg, size 6, beaten
30 ml (2 tbsp) chopped fresh coriander
150 ml (¼ pint) natural yogurt
lemon wedges and fresh coriander, to garnish

♦ Put 15 ml (1 tbsp) of the oil, the onion, carrot, garlic and ginger in a medium bowl. Cover with cling film, pulling back one corner to let steam escape, and microwave on HIGH for 5–7 minutes or until the vegetables have softened, stirring occasionally.

♦ Stir in the coriander and cumin seeds and microwave on HIGH for 1 minute, stirring occasionally.

♦ Stir in the nuts and microwave on HIGH for 2 minutes, stirring once.

♦ Stir in the cheese and breadcrumbs and season with salt and pepper. Mix thoroughly and bind together with the egg.

♦ Heat a browning dish for 8–10 minutes.

♦ Meanwhile, divide the mixture into six and shape into burgers. When the browning dish is hot, add the remaining oil and microwave on HIGH for 30 seconds.

♦ Quickly put the burgers in the dish and microwave on HIGH for 1½ minutes, then turn over and microwave on HIGH for a further minute or until browned. Leave to stand for 1 minute.

♦ Meanwhile, make the coriander raita. Beat the chopped coriander into the yogurt and season with salt and pepper.

♦ Garnish the burgers with lemon wedges and coriander and serve hot with the coriander raita.

photograph opposite page 65

opposite: Lentil, Mint and Yogurt Salad (see page 38)

LETTUCE DOLMAS
WITH TOMATO SAUCE

SERVES 2

♦ Wash the potatoes and prick all over with a fork. Arrange in a circle on absorbent kitchen paper and microwave on HIGH for 8–10 minutes, or until the potatoes are cooked, turning them over once during cooking.

♦ Meanwhile, conventionally hard-boil one of the eggs.

♦ Put the butter in a medium bowl and microwave on HIGH for 45 seconds or until melted. Stir in half of the onion and the garlic and microwave on HIGH for 3–4 minutes, or until softened.

♦ Halve the potatoes and scoop out the flesh. Stir the flesh into the onion and mash together. Stir in the parsley and season well with salt and pepper.

♦ Chop the hard-boiled egg and stir into the potato mixture. Beat the remaining egg and use to bind the potato mixture together.

♦ Wash and dry the lettuce leaves. Trim off any large stalks. Divide the potato mixture between the lettuce leaves, and roll up to form 6 neat parcels.

♦ Arrange in a single layer in a shallow dish with 15 ml (1 tbsp) water. Cover with cling film, pulling back one corner to let steam escape. Set aside.

♦ Put the remaining onion, tomatoes and their juice, bay leaf, parsley, sugar and marjoram into a medium bowl and microwave on HIGH for 5–7 minutes or until reduced and thickened. Allow to cool a little, then purée in a blender or food processor.

♦ Microwave the lettuce dolmas on HIGH for 4–6 minutes or until the lettuce has just softened and the filling is hot. Leave to stand for 2 minutes.

♦ Meanwhile, microwave the tomato sauce on HIGH for 1–2 minutes or until hot. Serve immediately with the dolmas, garnished with parsley.

3 old potatoes, about 175 g (6 oz) each
2 eggs
25 g (1 oz) butter or margarine, cut into pieces
1 medium onion, skinned and chopped
1 small garlic clove, skinned and crushed
30 ml (2 tbsp) chopped fresh parsley
salt and pepper
6 large round lettuce leaves
226 g (8 oz) can tomatoes
1 bay leaf
sprig of parsley
2.5 ml (½ level tsp) sugar
2.5 ml (½ level tsp) dried marjoram
parsley sprigs, to garnish

opposite: Chilled Courgette Mousse with Saffron Sauce (see page 46)

STUFFED PEPPERS AND TOMATOES

SERVES 2

1 green pepper
4 medium tomatoes
15 ml (1 tbsp) vegetable oil
1 small onion, skinned and chopped
1 garlic clove, skinned and crushed
10 ml (2 level tsp) tomato purée
5 ml (1 level tsp) paprika
100 g (4 oz) lean minced beef
30 ml (2 tbsp) chopped fresh mint
50 ml (2 fl oz) hot beef stock
salt and pepper
fresh mint, to garnish

♦ Cut the pepper in half lengthways and remove the seeds. Cut a slice off the top of each tomato and scoop out the pulp. Roughly chop the pulp and the lids.

♦ Put the oil, onion and garlic into a medium bowl and cover with cling film, pulling back one corner to let steam escape. Microwave on HIGH for 4–5 minutes or until softened.

♦ Stir in the tomato purée, paprika, minced beef, chopped tomato, mint, stock, salt and pepper. Microwave on HIGH for 8–10 minutes or until the beef is cooked and the sauce is slightly reduced.

♦ Put the pepper into a shallow dish with 30 ml (2 tbsp) water. Cover with cling film, pulling back one corner to let steam escape. Microwave on HIGH for 3–5 minutes or until tender. Drain.

♦ Stuff the pepper halves and the tomatoes with the mince mixture and return to the shallow dish.

♦ Microwave on HIGH for 3–5 minutes or until the peppers are really tender and the filling reheated. Serve each person with one pepper half and two tomatoes. Garnish with mint and serve hot.

CHEESE IN VINE LEAVES

SERVES 2

10 pickled vine leaves
225 g (8 oz) feta cheese
45 ml (3 tbsp) olive or vegetable oil
10 ml (2 tsp) lemon juice
7.5 ml (½ tbsp) chopped fresh coriander
7.5 ml (½ tbsp) chopped fresh mint
salt and pepper
6 thin slices of French bread, toasted
lemon twists, coriander and mint, to garnish

♦ Thoroughly rinse the vine leaves and put into a large bowl. Pour over enough boiling water to cover.

♦ Cover with cling film, pulling back one corner to let steam escape, and microwave on HIGH for 15 minutes, stirring occasionally. Leave to stand for 5 minutes, then rinse thoroughly. Drain and pat dry.

♦ Cut the cheese into 8 neat cubes. Spread 8 of the vine leaves out on a flat surface and place a piece of cheese about 2.5 cm (1 inch) away from the base of each leaf.

♦ Fold the sides of the leaf over the cheese, tucking the edges in. Roll up to form 8 small, neat parcels.

♦ Arrange the wrapped cheeses in a small shallow dish which is just large enough to hold them in a single layer.

♦ Mix the oil, lemon juice and herbs together, season well with salt and pepper and pour over the parcels, making sure that each parcel is covered with some dressing. Cover with the remaining vine leaves and microwave on HIGH for 1–1½ minutes or until the parcels feel slightly soft.

♦ Arrange the toast on two serving plates and top with the vine leaves which were used as a cover. Arrange the cheese parcels on top and spoon over the cooking liquid.

♦ Serve immediately, garnished with lemon twists, coriander and mint.

SPINACH TARTS WITH TOMATO AND BASIL SALAD

SERVES 2

♦ Mix the flour and a pinch of salt in a bowl. Cut half of the butter into small pieces and add it to the flour.

♦ Rub in the butter until the mixture resembles fine breadcrumbs, then make a well in the centre and stir in one of the egg yolks and 15–30 ml (1–2 tbsp) water. Mix together using a round bladed knife. Knead lightly to give a firm, smooth dough.

♦ Roll out the dough thinly. Invert two 10 cm (4 inch) shallow glass flan dishes and cover the base and sides with the dough. Cover with cling film and chill while making the filling.

♦ Put the remaining butter in a large bowl and microwave on HIGH for 1 minute or until melted.

♦ Stir in the onion and garlic and cover with cling film, pulling back one corner to let steam escape. Microwave on HIGH for 4–5 minutes or until softened.

♦ Add the spinach, cover again and microwave on HIGH for 8–9 minutes or until thawed, stirring frequently.

♦ Stir in 60 ml (4 tbsp) of the Parmesan cheese, the cream and season well with salt, pepper and nutmeg.

♦ Remove the cling film from the pastry cases and prick all over with a fork. Microwave on HIGH, pastry side uppermost, for 2–2½ minutes or until the pastry is firm to the touch. Leave to stand for 4–5 minutes, then carefully invert the pastry cases on to a wire rack. Remove the flan dishes and leave the pastry cases to crisp.

♦ Meanwhile, thinly slice the tomatoes and arrange on two large serving plates. Sprinkle with the basil and drizzle over the olive oil. Season with salt and pepper.

♦ Microwave the spinach filling on HIGH for 2–3 minutes, stirring occasionally, then stir in the remaining egg yolk and microwave on HIGH for 1–1½ minutes or until slightly thickened.

♦ Transfer the pastry cases to the serving plates and carefully spoon in the spinach filling. Sprinkle with the remaining Parmesan and serve immediately.

photograph opposite page 64

50 g (2 oz) plain wholemeal flour
salt and pepper
50 g (2 oz) butter or margarine
2 egg yolks
1 small onion, skinned and finely chopped
1 small garlic clove, skinned and crushed
300 g (10.6 oz) packet frozen leaf spinach
75 ml (5 level tbsp) grated Parmesan cheese
60 ml (4 tbsp) double cream
freshly grated nutmeg
3 large tomatoes
15 ml (1 tbsp) chopped fresh basil
15 ml (1 tbsp) olive or vegetable oil

WARM SPINACH AND CHICKEN LIVER SALAD WITH CROUTONS

SERVES 1

15 g (½ oz) butter or margarine
½ garlic clove, skinned and crushed
salt and pepper
1 thick slice wholemeal bread
100 g (4 oz) young spinach, washed and trimmed
100 g (4 oz) chicken livers
30 ml (2 tbsp) vegetable oil
10 ml (2 tsp) white wine vinegar

♦ Put the butter in a small bowl and beat until soft. Beat in the garlic and salt and pepper. Remove the crusts from the bread and spread on both sides with the garlic butter.

♦ Cut into 1 cm (½ inch) cubes, arrange in a circle on a sheet of greaseproof paper and set aside.

♦ Shred any large spinach leaves, but leave small leaves whole and arrange in an individual serving bowl.

♦ Chop the chicken livers into small pieces, cutting away any ducts and gristle.

♦ Put the oil into a medium bowl and microwave on HIGH for 30 seconds. Stir in the chicken livers and cover with cling film, pulling back one corner to let steam escape. Microwave on HIGH for 1½–2 minutes or until just cooked, stirring occasionally.

♦ Stir in the vinegar, salt and pepper and leave to stand while cooking the croûtons.

♦ Microwave the croûtons, on the greaseproof paper, on HIGH for 1–2 minutes or until firm, turning once. Leave to stand for 1 minute.

♦ Reheat the chicken livers, if necessary, for 30 seconds only. Pour quickly on to the spinach and toss together until well mixed.

♦ Sprinkle the croûtons on top and serve immediately.

TO SERVE 2

Double the ingredients.
In Point 3: Arrange the spinach leaves in two individual serving bowls.
In Point 5: Microwave the oil on HIGH for 45 seconds, then stir in the chicken livers and microwave on HIGH for 2–3 minutes or until just cooked.
In Point 7: Micorwave on HIGH for 2 minutes or until firm, turning once. Leave to stand for 1–2 minutes.

FISH STUFFED COURGETTES
WITH TARRAGON SAUCE

SERVES 2

♦ Trim the courgettes and cut in half lengthways. Arrange in a single layer in a shallow dish.

♦ Pour over 60 ml (4 tbsp) water and cover with cling film, pulling back one corner to let steam escape. Microwave on HIGH for 8–10 minutes or until just cooked.

♦ Drain the courgettes, reserving the cooking liquid. With a teaspoon, scoop out the flesh into a bowl, leaving a thin shell. Mash the flesh, pouring off any excess liquid.

♦ Put the fish in a shallow dish with the milk. Cover with cling film, pulling back one corner to let steam escape, and microwave on HIGH for 2–3 minutes or until the fish is cooked. Drain, skin and flake the fish, reserving the cooking liquid.

♦ Mix the flaked fish with the courgette flesh, garlic, salt and pepper. Bind together with the egg yolk.

♦ Sandwich the courgette shells together with the stuffing and put on to two serving plates. Set aside.

♦ Put the oil and flour in a small bowl and microwave on HIGH for 1 minute. Gradually stir in the wine and the reserved cooking liquids. Stir in the tarragon, salt and pepper.

♦ Microwave on HIGH for 4–5 minutes, whisking frequently. Leave to stand.

♦ Meanwhile, microwave the stuffed courgettes, one plate at a time, for 2 minutes each or until hot. Cover to keep warm

♦ Reheat the sauce on HIGH for 1 minute, if necessary. Garnish the stuffed courgettes with tarragon and serve immediately with the sauce.

4 medium courgettes
225 g (8 oz) haddock or cod fillet
45 ml (3 tbsp) milk
1 small garlic clove, skinned and crushed
salt and pepper
1 egg yolk, beaten
15 ml (1 tbsp) vegetable oil
10 ml (2 level tsp) plain flour
150 ml (¼ pint) medium dry white wine
15 ml (1 tbsp) chopped fresh tarragon or 5 ml (1 level tsp) dried
fresh tarragon, to garnish

SCAMPI AND BACON KEBABS

SERVES 2

40 g (1½ oz) butter or margarine, cut into small pieces
1 garlic clove, skinned and crushed
15 ml (1 tbsp) chopped fresh parsley
5 ml (1 tsp) lemon juice
salt and pepper
4 rashers smoked streaky bacon, rinded
175 g (6 oz) scampi
chopped fresh parsley, to garnish

◆ Put the butter and garlic in a shallow rectangular dish and microwave on HIGH for 1 minute or until the butter has melted.

◆ Stir in the parsley and lemon juice and season with salt and pepper. Microwave on HIGH for 1 minute, stirring once.

◆ Stretch the bacon rashers, using the back of a knife, and cut in half widthways.

◆ Thread the bacon and the scampi on to eight wooden skewers, winding the bacon under and over the scampi.

◆ Dip the kebabs in the garlic butter and arrange in a single layer in the dish.

◆ Cover loosely with a double thickness of absorbent kitchen paper and microwave on HIGH for 4–5 minutes, or until the bacon is cooked, repositioning once during cooking.

◆ Serve four kebabs each, with the garlic butter poured over and garnished with parsley.

MONKFISH AND MANGE-TOUT SAUTE

SERVES 2

350 g (12 oz) monkfish or cod fillet
15 ml (1 tbsp) vegetable oil
finely grated rind and juice of ½ lemon
1.25 ml (¼ level tsp) fennel seeds
75 g (3 oz) mange-tout
15 ml (1 tbsp) chopped fresh mixed herbs or a pinch of dried
salt and pepper
crusty brown bread, to serve

◆ Cut the fish into 2.5 cm (1 inch) cubes.

◆ Put the fish, oil, lemon rind and juice, and the fennel seeds in a medium bowl. Microwave on HIGH for 2 minutes, stirring once.

◆ Top and tail the mange-tout and cut in half. Stir into the fish with the mixed herbs and add salt and pepper to taste. Microwave on HIGH for 1–2 minutes or until the fish is tender, stirring once.

◆ Serve immediately, with crusty brown bread, if liked.

SPICY BUTTERFLY PRAWNS

♦ Remove the shells from the prawns, leaving the tail shells intact.
♦ With kitchen scissors, split the prawns along the inner curve, stopping at the tail shell, and cutting deep enough to expose the dark vein.
♦ Spread each prawn wide open, remove the dark vein, then rinse under cold running water. Dry thoroughly on absorbent kitchen paper.
♦ Put the butter in a medium bowl and microwave on HIGH for 45 seconds or until melted.
♦ Stir in the remaining ingredients and mix together well. Add the prawns and stir to coat in the spices.
♦ Leave to marinate in a cool place for at least 30 minutes.
♦ To cook the prawns, cover with cling film pulling back one corner to let steam escape. Microwave on HIGH for 2–3 minutes or until the prawns change colour, stirring occasionally. Serve hot, garnished with lime wedges.

8 medium raw prawns, in the shell
15 g (½ oz) butter or margarine, cut into pieces
1 garlic clove, skinned and crushed
juice of ½ lime
1 cm (½ inch) piece of fresh root ginger, peeled and finely chopped
2.5 ml (½ level tsp) ground cumin
2.5 ml (½ level tsp) ground cardamom
5 ml (1 level tsp) ground turmeric
5 ml (1 level tsp) paprika
pinch of mild chilli powder
salt
lime wedges, to garnish

FISH TERRINE WITH BASIL SAUCE

♦ Grease two 11×7.5 cm (4½×3 inch), 350 ml (12 fl oz) ovenproof containers and line the base with greaseproof paper.
♦ Cut the whiting into small pieces, put in a blender or food processor and blend until finely chopped.
♦ Gradually add the egg white, lemon juice, salt and pepper and blend until smooth.
♦ Turn into a bowl and stir in the dill and a third of the basil. Gradually beat in half of the soured cream. Cover and chill for 15 minutes.
♦ Skin the salmon and cut into 1 cm (½ inch) cubes. Carefully stir into the fish mixture.
♦ Spoon into the lined container and carefully level the surface with a knife.
♦ Loosely cover with absorbent kitchen paper and microwave on LOW for 6½–7 minutes or until the mixture feels firm and shrinks slightly away from the edges of the containers.
♦ Leave to cool for about 30 minutes, then chill for at least 30 minutes.
♦ When ready to serve, make the sauce. Mix the remaining soured cream with a little milk to make a thin sauce. Stir in the remaining basil, salt and pepper.
♦ To serve, turn out the terrines and wipe with absorbent kitchen paper to remove any excess liquid.
♦ Coat two individual serving plates with the sauce and place a terrine in the centre of each. Garnish with basil and serve immediately.

225 g (8 oz) whiting, sole or plaice fillet, skinned
1 egg white, size 6, chilled
5 ml (1 tsp) lemon juice
salt and pepper
5 ml (1 tsp) chopped fresh dill or 2.5 ml (½ level tsp) dried
25 ml (1½ tbsp) chopped fresh basil or 5 ml (1 level tsp) dried
150 ml (¼ pint) soured cream, chilled
100 g (4 oz) piece of fresh salmon tail fillet
a little milk
basil sprigs, to garnish

STUFFED PLAICE TIMBALES WITH LEMON HERB BUTTER

SERVES 1

15 g (½ oz) butter
2.5 ml (½ tsp) lemon juice
15 ml (1 tbsp) chopped fresh parsley
salt and pepper
75 g (3 oz) mushrooms
15 ml (1 tbsp) vegetable oil
40 g (1½ oz) long grain rice
150 ml (¼ pint) hot chicken stock
1 large double plaice fillet, skinned
lemon twists and fresh parsley, to garnish

◆ To make the lemon herb butter, put the butter into a small bowl and beat until soft. Add the lemon juice, half of the parsley and season well with salt and pepper. Beat together well. Push to the side of the bowl to form a small pat and chill while making the timbales.

◆ Finely chop the mushrooms and put into a medium bowl with the oil. Cover with cling film, pulling back one corner to let steam escape, and microwave on HIGH for 1–1½ minutes or until the mushrooms have softened.

◆ Stir in the rice and the chicken stock, cover again and microwave on HIGH for 8–10 minutes, or until the rice is tender and the stock has been absorbed, stirring occasionally.

◆ Meanwhile, cut the plaice fillet in half lengthways, to make two long fillets.

◆ Place 1 fillet, skinned side in, around the inside of each of 2 buttered 150 ml (¼ pint) ramekin or individual soufflé dishes. The fish should line the dish leaving a hole in the centre.

◆ When the rice is cooked, stir in the remaining parsley and salt and pepper to taste. Spoon this mixture into the centre of each ramekin, pressing down well.

◆ Cover loosely with cling film and microwave on HIGH for 1½–2 minutes or until the fish is cooked.

◆ Leave to stand for 2–3 minutes, then invert the ramekin dishes on to serving plates. With the dishes still in place pour off any excess liquid, then carefully remove the dishes.

◆ Garnish the plaice timbales with lemon twists and parsley and serve hot, with a knob of lemon butter on top of each.

TO SERVE 2

Double the ingredients.
In Point 2: Cook the mushrooms on HIGH for 2–3 minutes or until the mushrooms are softened.
In Point 3: Cook the rice on HIGH for 10–12 minutes or until tender.
In Point 7: Cook the fish on HIGH for 2–3 minutes or until cooked.

PRAWN AND MUSHROOM SCALLOPS

SERVES 1

◆ Wash and scrub the potatoes, and prick all over with a fork. Place on absorbent kitchen paper and microwave on HIGH for 8–10 minutes or until soft, turning over once during cooking. Set aside.

◆ Put 150 ml (¼ pint) of the milk, the flour and half of the butter into a medium bowl and microwave on HIGH for 2–3 minutes, whisking frequently, until boiling and thickened.

◆ Stir in the mushrooms and microwave on HIGH for 2 minutes, whisking occasionally. Season well with salt, pepper and nutmeg. Stir in the prawns and parsley and spoon into two scallop shells or individual gratin dishes.

◆ Cut the potatoes in half and scoop out the flesh. Mix with the remaining milk, butter, salt and pepper and beat until smooth and creamy. Spoon a potato border around each scallop shell or gratin dish.

◆ Microwave on HIGH for 2–3 minutes or until heated through. Brown under a preheated grill, if desired, and garnish with chopped parsley. Serve immediately with a green salad, if liked.

2 medium old potatoes, about 175 g (6 oz) each
200 ml (7 fl oz) milk
30 ml (2 level tbsp) plain flour
25 g (1 oz) butter or margarine
75 g (3 oz) button mushrooms, sliced
salt and pepper
freshly grated nutmeg
50 g (2 oz) peeled prawns
15 ml (1 tbsp) chopped fresh parsley
chopped parsley, to garnish

SEA SHELLS WITH ANCHOVY AND PARSLEY DRESSING

SERVES 1

◆ Put the pasta and salt to taste in a medium bowl. Pour over 600 ml (1 pint) boiling water. Stir and microwave on HIGH for 6–8 minutes or until almost tender, stirring occasionally. Leave to stand while making the dressing. Do not drain.

◆ To make the dressing, put the lemon juice and garlic in a small bowl and stir in the anchovy fillets, parsley and pepper.

◆ Drain the pasta and rinse with boiling water. Turn the pasta into a warmed serving dish and toss in the butter. Pour the dressing over and toss together, making sure that all the pasta is coated in dressing. Serve immediately.

TO SERVE 2

Double the ingredients.
In Point 1: Put the pasta and salt to taste in a large bowl and pour over 1.1 litres (2 pints) boiling water. Microwave on HIGH for 12–14 minutes or until almost tender, stirring occasionally.

100 g (4 oz) medium dried pasta shells
salt and pepper
15 ml (1 tbsp) lemon juice
1 small garlic clove, skinned and crushed
6–8 anchovy fillets, drained and roughly chopped
30 ml (2 tbsp) chopped fresh parsley
40 g (1½ oz) butter

MUSSELS IN CREAM
AND GARLIC SAUCE

SERVES 1

450 g (1 lb) fresh mussels
75 ml (3 fl oz) dry white wine
½ small onion, skinned and finely chopped
1 garlic clove, skinned and crushed
75 ml (3 fl oz) double cream
5 ml (1 tsp) lemon juice
pinch of ground turmeric
salt and pepper
1 egg yolk, size 6
chopped fresh parsley, to garnish

◆ To clean mussels, put them in a sink or bowl and scrub thoroughly with a hard brush. Wash in several changes of water.

◆ Scrape off any 'beards' or tufts protruding from the shells, then leave the mussels to soak in a bowl of cold water for 20 minutes.

◆ Discard any mussels that are not tightly closed, or do not close if tapped with a knife.

◆ Drain, and put into a large bowl with the wine and onion. Cover with cling film, pulling back one corner to let steam escape, and microwave on HIGH for 4–5 minutes or until all the mussels have opened, stirring once. Discard any mussels which do not open.

◆ Strain the mussels through a sieve and return the cooking liquid to the bowl. Keep the mussels warm while making the sauce.

◆ Stir the garlic into the reserved cooking liquid and microwave on HIGH for 4–5 minutes, until reduced by half.

◆ Stir in the cream, lemon juice, turmeric, salt and pepper and microwave on HIGH for 2 minutes or until hot.

◆ Stir in the egg yolk and microwave on HIGH for 30 seconds or until slightly thickened, stirring occasionally.

◆ Pour the sauce over the mussels, sprinkle with chopped parsley and serve immediately.

TO SERVE 2

Double the ingredients, using one size 2 egg yolk instead of size 6.

In Point 4: Cook the mussels in two batches so the timing remains the same.

In Point 5: Pour the cooking liquids into one bowl.

In Point 6: Microwave on HIGH for 5–6 minutes or until reduced by half.

In Point 8: Microwave on HIGH for 30 seconds–1 minute or until slightly thickened.

CHICKEN WITH APPLE AND CURRIED MAYONNAISE

SERVES 1

♦ Put the onion, chicken breast, wine, bay leaf, mixed herbs and salt and pepper in a shallow dish. Cover with cling film, pulling back one corner to let steam escape, and microwave on HIGH for 3–4 minutes or until tender.
♦ Cut the chicken into bite-sized pieces and set aside. Stir the curry powder into the cooking liquid and microwave on HIGH for 1–2 minutes or until slightly reduced.
♦ Meanwhile, core, seed and dice the green pepper and core and thinly slice the apple. Mix with the chicken, stir in the lemon juice and set aside.
♦ Stir the mayonnaise and apricot jam into the cooking liquid and season with salt and pepper. Pour over the chicken mixture and mix together until thoroughly coated.
♦ Line a serving dish with the lettuce leaves and pile in the chicken mayonnaise. Chill for about 20 minutes before serving.

TO SERVE 2

Double the ingredients.
In Point 1: Microwave on HIGH for 5–6 minutes or until the chicken is tender.
In Point 2: Microwave on HIGH for 2–3 minutes or until slightly reduced.

1 small onion, skinned and chopped
1 chicken breast fillet, skinned
30 ml (2 tbsp) dry white wine
1 bay leaf
large pinch dried mixed herbs
salt and pepper
10 ml (2 level tsp) mild curry powder
½ small green pepper
½ small red apple
5 ml (1 tsp) lemon juice
45 ml (3 tbsp) mayonnaise
10 ml (2 tsp) apricot jam
few lettuce leaves, to serve

MAIN DISHES

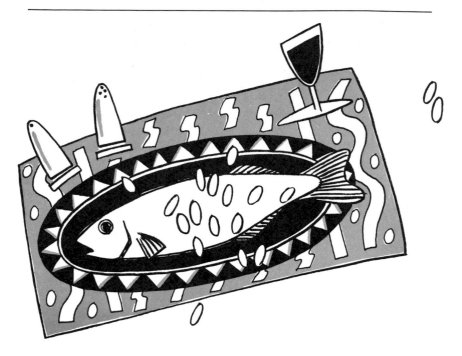

BEEF WITH GINGER AND GARLIC

SERVES 2

350 g (12 oz) fillet steak, trimmed of fat and sliced
2.5 cm (1 inch) piece of fresh root ginger, peeled and finely grated
1 garlic clove, skinned and crushed
150 ml (¼ pint) dry sherry
30 ml (2 tbsp) soy sauce
2 medium carrots
15 ml (1 tbsp) vegetable oil
30 ml (2 level tbsp) cornflour
2.5 ml (½ level tsp) soft brown sugar

♦ Cut the steak across the grain into 1 cm (½ inch) strips, and put into a medium bowl.

♦ Mix the ginger with the garlic, sherry and soy sauce. Pour over the steak, making sure that all the meat is coated, cover and leave to marinate for at least 30 minutes.

♦ Peel the carrots, and cut them into thin slices lengthways, using a potato peeler.

♦ Put the oil in a large bowl and microwave on HIGH for 1 minute or until hot.

♦ Remove the steak from the marinade using a slotted spoon and stir into the hot oil. Microwave on HIGH for 1–2 minutes, or until the steak is just cooked, stirring once.

♦ Meanwhile, blend the cornflour and the sugar with a little of the marinade to make a smooth paste, then gradually blend in all of the marinade.

♦ Stir the carrots into the steak and microwave on HIGH for 1–2 minutes, then gradually stir in the cornflour and marinade mixture.

♦ Microwave on HIGH for 2–3 minutes, until boiling and thickened, stirring frequently. Serve immediately with boiled rice, if liked.

COTTAGE PIE

SERVES 1

♦ Prick the potatoes all over with a fork and place on absorbent kitchen paper. Microwave on HIGH for 8–10 minutes or until the potatoes are cooked, turning them over once during cooking. Set aside.

♦ Put the onion, carrot and the oil in an individual flameproof serving dish, cover with cling film, pulling back one corner to let steam escape, and microwave on HIGH for 3–4 minutes or until softened, stirring occasionally.

♦ Stir in the beef and microwave on HIGH for 2 minutes or until the meat changes colour, stirring occasionally to break up the mince.

♦ Stir in the Worcestershire sauce, stock, tomato purée, salt and pepper. Microwave on HIGH for 5–7 minutes or until the meat is tender, stirring occasionally.

♦ Meanwhile, halve the potatoes and scoop out the flesh. Turn into a bowl and mash with the parsley, butter, half of the cheese, salt and pepper.

♦ When the meat is cooked, spoon the mashed potato on top and rough the surface with a fork. Sprinkle with the remaining cheese.

♦ Microwave on HIGH for 2 minutes, or until the potato is hot and the cheese melted.

♦ Brown under a preheated grill if desired.

2 old potatoes, about 175 g (6 oz) each
1 small onion, skinned and finely chopped
1 small carrot, peeled and grated
10 ml (2 tsp) vegetable oil
175 g (6 oz) lean minced beef
5 ml (1 tsp) Worcestershire sauce
45 ml (3 tbsp) beef stock
2.5 ml (½ level tsp) tomato purée
salt and pepper
15 ml (1 tbsp) chopped fresh parsley
15 g (½ oz) butter or margarine
40 g (1½ oz) Cheddar cheese, grated

TO SERVE 2

Double the ingredients.

In Point 1: Arrange the potatoes in a circle and microwave on HIGH for 10–15 minutes or until tender.

In Point 2: Cook the onion, carrot and oil in a medium bowl and microwave on HIGH for 5–7 minutes or until tender.

In Point 3: Microwave the meat on HIGH for 2–3 minutes or until it changes colour.

In Point 4: Stir in the Worcestershire sauce, stock, tomato purée and seasoning and microwave on HIGH for 8–10 minutes or until the meat is tender.

In Point 6: Spoon the meat into two individual flameproof serving dishes, then divide the potato between the two dishes.

CHILLI CON CARNE

SERVES 2

1 medium onion, skinned and finely chopped
1 garlic clove, skinned and crushed
1 small green pepper, seeded and chopped
15 ml (1 tbsp) vegetable oil
5 ml (1 level tsp) ground cinnamon
10 ml (2 level tsp) ground coriander
5–10 ml (1–2 level tsp) mild chilli powder
350 g (12 oz) lean minced beef
226 g (8 oz) can tomatoes
15 ml (1 level tbsp) tomato purée
10 ml (2 tsp) red wine vinegar
salt and pepper
200 g (7 oz) can red kidney beans, drained
15 ml (1 tbsp) chopped fresh coriander (optional)

♦ Put the onion, garlic, green pepper, oil and spices in a medium bowl. Cover with cling film, pulling back one corner to let steam escape, and microwave on HIGH for 5–7 minutes, or until the onion has softened, stirring occasionally.
♦ Stir in the meat, tomatoes and their juice, tomato purée, vinegar, salt and pepper. Microwave on HIGH for 15–20 minutes, or until the meat is tender, stirring occasionally.
♦ Rinse the kidney beans and stir into the meat with the fresh coriander, if using. Microwave on HIGH for 5 minutes, stirring once. Serve hot, with rice or bread, if liked.

STEAK AND KIDNEY PUDDING

SERVES 2

100 g (4 oz) wholemeal self raising flour
large pinch of ground mace
15 ml (1 tbsp) chopped fresh parsley
50 g (2 oz) shredded suet
salt and pepper
1 egg, beaten
15 ml (1 tbsp) vegetable oil
1 medium onion, skinned and chopped
225 g (8 oz) rump steak, cut into thin strips
1–2 lamb's kidneys, skinned, halved, cored and chopped
30 ml (2 level tbsp) plain flour
150 ml (¼ pint) red wine
1 bay leaf

♦ To make the pastry, put the flour, mace, parsley, suet, salt and pepper into a bowl and mix together. Make a well in the centre, then stir in the egg and 30–45 ml (2–3 tbsp) cold water to make a soft, light elastic dough. Knead until smooth.
♦ Roll out two thirds of the pastry on a floured surface and use to line a 600 ml (1 pint) pudding basin.
♦ Put the oil and onion in a medium bowl, cover with cling film and pull back one corner to let steam escape. Microwave on HIGH for 5–7 minutes or until the onion is softened.
♦ Toss the steak and the chopped kidneys in the flour and stir into the softened onion. Microwave on HIGH for 3 minutes, then stir in the wine, bay leaf, salt and pepper.
♦ Recover and microwave on HIGH for 5 minutes, stirring occasionally.
♦ Spoon the mixture into the lined pudding basin. Roll out the remaining pastry to a circle to fit the top of the pudding. Dampen the edges and press firmly together to seal.
♦ Cover loosely with cling film and microwave on HIGH for 5 minutes, or until the pastry looks 'set'.
♦ Leave to stand for 5 minutes, then turn out on to a warmed serving dish or wrap a clean table napkin round the bowl and serve from the bowl. Serve immediately.

SPICY MINI MEATBALLS WITH TOMATO AND CORIANDER SAUCE

SERVES 2

◆ Put the onion, garlic and ginger in a blender or food processor and blend until very finely chopped.	*1 small onion, skinned and quartered*
◆ Add the beef, chutney, cumin, ground coriander and half the fresh chopped coriander and season with salt and pepper. Pour in the egg and blend until well mixed. Shape into 16 small balls.	*1 garlic clove, skinned and crushed*
	2.5 cm (1 inch) piece of fresh root ginger, peeled and crushed
◆ Arrange in a single layer in a shallow dish. Microwave on HIGH for 5–6 minutes or until cooked, rearranging once during cooking. Leave to stand, covered, while making the sauce.	*350 g (12 oz) lean minced beef*
	15 ml (1 level tbsp) mango chutney
◆ To make the sauce, put the tomatoes and their juice into a large bowl. Stir in the chicken stock, tomato purée, sugar, salt and pepper.	*2.5 ml (½ level tsp) ground cumin*
	2.5 ml (½ level tsp) ground coriander
◆ Microwave on HIGH for 5 minutes, stirring occasionally, then stir in the remaining fresh coriander and microwave on HIGH for 2–3 minutes or until reduced and thickened.	*30 ml (2 tbsp) chopped fresh coriander*
	salt and pepper
◆ Microwave the meatballs on HIGH for 1–2 minutes, or until reheated.	*1 egg, size 6, beaten*
◆ Serve the meatballs with the sauce, garnished with coriander.	*226 g (8 oz) can tomatoes*
	15 ml (1 tbsp) chicken stock
	10 ml (2 level tsp) tomato purée
	5 ml (1 level tsp) granulated sugar
	fresh coriander, to garnish

photograph opposite page 80

LAMB CHOPS WITH ROSEMARY AND GARLIC

SERVES 1

◆ Preheat a browning dish for 8–10 minutes.	*5 ml (1 tsp) vegetable oil*
◆ Add the oil, then quickly add the chops. Microwave on HIGH for 2 minutes, then turn over and microwave on HIGH for 1 minute or until cooked as desired.	*2 lamb loin chops*
	knob of butter
◆ Transfer the chops to a warmed serving dish. Stir the remaining ingredients into the browning dish and microwave on HIGH for 1½ minutes until golden brown. Pour over the chops, garnish with rosemary and serve immediately.	*½ small garlic clove, skinned and crushed*
	2.5 ml (½ tsp) finely chopped fresh rosemary or a pinch of dried
	salt and pepper

TO SERVE 2

Double the ingredients.	*5 ml (1 tsp) lemon juice*
In Point 2: Microwave on HIGH for 2½ minutes, then turn over and microwave on HIGH for 1½ minutes or until cooked as desired.	*fresh rosemary, to garnish*

MOUSSAKA

SERVES 2

1 small aubergine, about 275 g (10 oz)
salt and pepper
1 small onion, skinned and chopped
1 garlic clove, skinned and crushed
15 ml (1 tbsp) olive oil
225 g (8 oz) minced lamb or beef
15 ml (1 tbsp) tomato purée
5 ml (1 level tsp) ground cinnamon
2.5 ml (½ level tsp) ground allspice
5 ml (1 level tsp) dried oregano
227 g (8 oz) can tomatoes
75 ml (3 fl oz) milk
150 ml (¼ pint) natural Greek yogurt
5 ml (1 level tsp) cornflour
1 egg, beaten
75 g (3 oz) Cheddar cheese, grated
freshly grated nutmeg

◆ Cut the aubergine into 0.5 cm (¼ inch) slices and place in a colander. Sprinkle with salt and leave for 30 minutes to degorge.

◆ Meanwhile, put the onion, garlic and oil in a medium bowl. Cover with cling film, pulling back one corner to let steam escape, and microwave on HIGH for 3–4 minutes or until the onion has softened.

◆ Stir in the meat, tomato purée, cinnamon, allspice, oregano and the tomatoes and their juice. Microwave on HIGH for 10–15 minutes or until the meat is tender, stirring occasionally. Skim off any excess fat.

◆ Meanwhile, rinse the aubergines and pat dry with absorbent kitchen paper. Arrange in a single layer in a shallow dish. Cover with cling film, pulling back one corner to let steam escape, and microwave on HIGH for 5 minutes or until softened.

◆ To make the topping, beat the milk, yogurt, cornflour, egg and half of the cheese together. Season generously with salt, pepper and nutmeg.

◆ Arrange the meat and aubergines in layers in a flameproof dish, then pour over the sauce. Sprinkle with the remaining cheese.

◆ Microwave on LOW for 15 minutes until the topping is just set.

◆ Leave to stand for 10 minutes, then brown under a preheated grill if desired. Serve hot with a mixed salad, if liked.

opposite: Spinach Tarts with Tomato and Basil Salad (see page 51)

INDIAN SPINACH AND LAMB CURRY

SERVES 2

♦ Put the garlic, ginger, mustard seeds, coriander seeds, turmeric, chilli powder, onion and 15 ml (1 tbsp) water in a blender or food processor and process until smooth.

♦ Put the oil in a large bowl and microwave on HIGH for 1 minute until hot. Stir in the onion and spice paste and microwave on HIGH for 2 minutes, stirring once.

♦ Stir in the frozen spinach and microwave on HIGH for 7–9 minutes, or until thawed, stirring occasionally.

♦ Cut the lamb into small cubes and stir into the spinach and onion mixture. Microwave on HIGH for 15–20 minutes or until the lamb is tender, stirring occasionally.

♦ Stir in the yogurt and season to taste with salt and pepper. Microwave on HIGH for 1–2 minutes or until heated through. Serve immediately with boiled rice, if liked.

1 garlic clove, skinned and roughly chopped
1 cm (½ inch) piece of fresh root ginger, peeled and roughly chopped
10 ml (2 level tsp) mustard seeds
10 ml (2 level tsp) coriander seeds
2.5 ml (½ level tsp) ground turmeric
pinch of chilli powder
1 large onion, skinned and roughly chopped
15 ml (1 tbsp) vegetable oil
350 g (12 oz) lamb fillet, trimmed
225 g (8 oz) frozen leaf spinach
150 ml (¼ pint) natural yogurt
salt and pepper

MINTED LAMB BURGERS WITH CUCUMBER

SERVES 2

♦ Preheat a browning dish for 8–10 minutes.

♦ Meanwhile mix together the lamb, onion, lemon rind and half of the mint sauce. Season with salt and pepper and bind together with the egg yolk.

♦ Divide the mixture into four, shape into burgers and coat in the flour. When the browning dish is hot, add the oil and microwave on HIGH for 30 seconds.

♦ Quickly put the burgers in the dish and microwave on HIGH for 1½ minutes, then turn over and microwave on HIGH for 2 minutes or until browned. Stir in any remaining flour.

♦ Cut the cucumber into 5 cm (2 inch) long wedges and the spring onions into 1 cm (½ inch) pieces. Add to the pan.

♦ Stir in the stock and sherry and the remaining mint and season with salt and pepper.

♦ Microwave on HIGH for 3 minutes or until the liquid is slightly reduced and the meat is tender. Skim off any excess fat, garnish with fresh mint and serve immediately with baked potatoes, if liked.

350 g (12 oz) raw minced lamb
1 small onion, skinned and finely chopped
finely grated rind of ½ a small lemon
10 ml (2 tsp) mint sauce
salt and pepper
1 egg yolk
15 ml (1 tbsp) flour
15 ml (1 tbsp) vegetable oil
½ a small cucumber
3 spring onions, trimmed
75 ml (3 fl oz) chicken stock
10 ml (2 tsp) sherry
fresh mint, to garnish

opposite: Spicy Nut Burgers with Coriander Raita (see page 48)

SPARERIBS WITH
REDCURRANT AND HONEY GLAZE

SERVES 1

1 small onion, skinned and very finely chopped
1 garlic clove, skinned and crushed
45 ml (3 level tbsp) redcurrant jelly
15 ml (1 tbsp) clear honey
15 ml (1 tbsp) soy sauce
15 ml (1 tbsp) red wine vinegar
dash of hot chilli sauce
salt and pepper
450 g (1 lb) Chinese-style pork spareribs
15 ml (1 level tbsp) cornflour

◆ Blend the onion, garlic, redcurrant jelly, honey, soy sauce and vinegar together in a large bowl. Season to taste with chilli sauce, salt and pepper.
◆ Stir in the ribs and coat in the marinade. Cover and leave in the refrigerator for at least 30 minutes for the ribs to absorb the flavour.
◆ Remove the ribs from the marinade, reserving the marinade for the sauce. Arrange the ribs in a single layer in a shallow dish. Cover with absorbent kitchen paper and microwave on HIGH for 5 minutes.
◆ Rearrange the ribs, then microwave on MEDIUM for 15–20 minutes or until tender, rearranging and turning once during cooking.
◆ Blend the cornflour with 5 ml (1 tsp) cold water to make a smooth paste, then stir into the reserved marinade.
◆ Pour over the ribs making sure that they are all covered, and microwave on HIGH for 5 minutes, or until the ribs are thoroughly glazed and the sauce thickened, basting occasionally during cooking.
◆ Serve hot, with a jacket potato and a green salad, if liked.

TO SERVE 2

Increase the cornflour to 45 ml (3 level tsp) and double the remaining ingredients.
In Point 4: Microwave on MEDIUM for 20–25 minutes or until tender.
In Point 6: Microwave on HIGH for 8–10 minutes or until thoroughly glazed and the sauce thickened.

PORK WITH HORSERADISH CREAM SAUCE

SERVES 2

♦ Preheat a browning dish for 8–10 minutes.

♦ Meanwhile, cut the pork into 1 cm (½ inch) slices. Place between two sheets of cling film and with a rolling pin flatten to a thickness of 0.5 cm (¼ inch).

♦ When the browning dish is ready, add the oil, garlic and the pork and microwave on HIGH for 2–3 minutes or until the pork is lightly browned on one side.

♦ Turn the pork over and microwave on HIGH for 1–2 minutes or until the second side is brown.

♦ Meanwhile, peel and grate the apple and mix with the horseradish, cream, lemon juice, salt and pepper.

♦ Add the cream mixture to the pork, stirring to loosen any sediment at the bottom of the dish.

♦ Microwave on HIGH for 2–3 minutes or until the pork is tender, stirring occasionally. Serve hot, garnished with apple slices.

350 g (12 oz) pork tenderloin or fillet
15 ml (1 tbsp) vegetable oil
1 garlic clove, skinned and crushed
1 small eating apple
30 ml (2 tbsp) creamed horseradish
150 ml (¼ pint) soured cream
5 ml (1 tsp) lemon juice
salt and pepper
apple slices, to garnish

MARINATED PORK WITH PEANUTS

SERVES 1

♦ Put the peanut butter in a small bowl and gradually mix in the soy sauce, lemon juice, chilli powder, cumin, sugar and garlic.

♦ Trim any excess fat from the pork and prick all over with a fork. Coat with the peanut mixture.

♦ Put into a shallow dish, cover loosely with cling film and leave in the refrigerator to marinate for at least 30 minutes.

♦ To cook the pork, pull back one corner of the cling film to let steam escape, and microwave on HIGH for 6–7 minutes or until tender, turning once during cooking. Leave to stand, covered, for 5 minutes.

♦ Meanwhile, cut the cucumber into 5 cm (2 inch) long strips, and arrange on a serving plate.

♦ Serve the pork with the cucumber garnish and boiled rice.

TO SERVE 2

Double the ingredients.
In Point 4: Microwave on HIGH for 7½–8½ minutes or until cooked. Leave to stand for 5 minutes.

30 ml (2 level tbsp) crunchy peanut butter
15 ml (1 tbsp) soy sauce
5 ml (1 tsp) lemon juice
1.25 ml (¼ level tsp) mild chilli powder
2.5 ml (½ level tsp) ground cumin
5 ml (1 level tsp) dark soft brown sugar
1 garlic clove, skinned and crushed
1 pork loin chop, about 2.5 cm (1 inch) thick
10 cm (4 inch) piece of cucumber, cut in half widthways
boiled rice, to serve

PORK WITH BLACKCURRANT SAUCE

SERVES 1

1 pork loin chop, about 2.5 cm (1 inch) thick
5 ml (1 level tsp) mild prepared mustard
150 ml (¼ pint) chicken stock
30 ml (2 level tbsp) blackcurrant preserve
salt and pepper
10 ml (2 tsp) white wine vinegar
watercress, to garnish

◆ Preheat a browning dish for 8–10 minutes.

◆ Meanwhile, trim the chop and remove the rind and all excess fat. Cut the fat into chunks and reserve.

◆ Gradually blend the mustard and the stock into the blackcurrant preserve and season with salt and pepper. Set aside.

◆ When the browning dish is ready, add the pork fat and microwave on HIGH for 1 minute or until the fat begins to run. Quickly add the pork chop and microwave on HIGH for 1½ minutes, or until browned.

◆ Turn the chop over and microwave on HIGH for 1 minute. Remove the pieces of fat.

◆ Stir in the blackcurrant mixture, cover with cling film, pulling back one corner to let steam escape, and microwave on HIGH for 3–4 minutes or until the chop is tender.

◆ Transfer the chop to a warmed serving plate, cover with foil and leave to stand.

◆ Skim off any excess fat from the sauce, add the vinegar and microwave on HIGH for 2–3 minutes, or until reduced and thickened, stirring once and carefully scraping the bottom of the browning dish to remove any sediment.

◆ Adjust the seasoning if necessary, and pour the sauce over the chop. Serve immediately, garnished with watercress.

TO SERVE 2

Use 200 ml (7 fl oz) chicken stock and 45 ml (3 level tbsp) blackcurrant preserve. Double the remaining ingredients.

In Point 4: Microwave the chops on HIGH for 2 minutes.

In Point 5: Turn over and microwave on HIGH for 2 minutes.

In Point 6: Microwave on HIGH for 5–6 minutes or until tender.

In Point 8: Microwave on HIGH for 3–4 minutes or until reduced and thickened.

KIDNEYS AND MUSHROOMS IN RED WINE

SERVES 1

♦ Put the oil and onion in a large shallow dish, cover with cling film, pulling back one corner to let steam escape, and microwave on HIGH for 3–4 minutes or until the onion has softened.

♦ Skin the kidneys and cut in halves lengthways. Snip out the cores with kitchen scissors. Add to the dish and microwave on HIGH for 2 minutes or until just changing colour, turning once.

♦ Sprinkle in the flour, then gradually add the wine, stock, bouquet garni, tomato purée, mushrooms, salt and pepper.

♦ Cover again and microwave on HIGH for 4–5 minutes, or until the kidneys are tender, stirring occasionally.

♦ Remove the bouquet garni, adjust seasoning, if necessary, and serve immediately, garnished with chopped parsley.

15 ml (1 tbsp) vegetable oil
1 small onion, skinned and finely chopped
3 lamb's kidneys
15 ml (1 level tbsp) plain flour
75 ml (3 fl oz) red wine
75 ml (3 fl oz) beef stock
bouquet garni
10 ml (2 level tsp) tomato purée
50 g (2 oz) mushrooms, sliced
salt and pepper
chopped fresh parsley, to garnish

TO SERVE 2

Use 150 ml (¼ pint) red wine and 100 ml (4 fl oz) beef stock and double all the remaining ingredients.

In Point 1: Microwave the onion on HIGH for 4–6 minutes or until softened.

In Point 2: Microwave the kidneys on HIGH for 3 minutes, or until just changing colour.

In Point 4: Microwave on HIGH for 6–7 minutes or until the kidneys are tender.

HERBY CHICKEN PARCEL

SERVES 1

75 ml (3 tbsp) Greek strained yogurt
salt and pepper
15 ml (1 tbsp) chopped fresh mixed herbs, such as tarragon, dill, chervil, parsley
1 chicken breast fillet, skinned
1 lemon slice

♦ Mix the yogurt, cornflour, salt and pepper together and stir in the herbs. Spread the mixture all over the chicken breast.

♦ Cut a 30.5 cm (12 inch) square of greaseproof paper and place the chicken breast on it. Lay the lemon slices on top of the chicken and season with more pepper.

♦ Fold the paper over the chicken to make a neat parcel, twisting the ends together to ensure that the juices do not escape.

♦ Microwave on LOW for 7–8 minutes or until the chicken is tender, turning the parcel over once during cooking. Serve in the parcel with rice, if liked.

TO SERVE 2

Double the ingredients.

In Point 4: Microwave on LOW for 10–12 minutes, or until the chicken is tender.

SHREDDED CHICKEN WITH MUSHROOMS AND POPPY SEEDS

SERVES 1

1 chicken breast fillet, skinned
50 g (2 oz) button mushrooms
4 cm (1½ inch) piece of cucumber
15 ml (1 tbsp) vegetable oil
2 spring onions, chopped
7.5 ml (1½ level tsp) cornflour
15 ml (1 tbsp) sherry
60 ml (4 tbsp) chicken stock
2.5 ml (½ tsp) white wine vinegar
5–10 ml (1–2 level tsp) black poppy seeds
spring onion tassels, to garnish

♦ Cut the chicken into thin strips and thinly slice the mushrooms. Cut the cucumber into thin strips.

♦ Put the oil into a medium bowl and stir in the chicken. Microwave on HIGH for 1–1½ minutes or until the chicken changes colour, stirring occasionally.

♦ Stir in the mushrooms, cucumber and onion and microwave on HIGH for 2 minutes.

♦ Meanwhile, blend the cornflour with the sherry, stock and wine vinegar. Stir in the poppy seeds.

♦ Stir the liquid into the chicken and mushrooms and microwave on HIGH for 3–4 minutes, or until the chicken is tender, stirring occasionally. Season with salt and pepper and serve immediately, garnished with spring onion tassels.

TO SERVE 2

Double the ingredients.

In Point 2: Microwave on HIGH for 1½–2 minutes, or until the chicken changes colour.

In Point 3: Microwave on HIGH for 3 minutes.

In Point 5: Microwave on HIGH for 5–6 minutes or until the chicken is tender, stirring occasionally.

CHICKEN, MANGO AND PISTACHIO NUT SALAD

SERVES 2

♦ Cut the chicken into bite-size pieces and put into a shallow dish with the oil.

♦ Cut the lime into thin slices and lay on top of the chicken.

♦ Cover with cling film, pulling back one corner to let steam escape, and microwave on HIGH for 2 minutes.

♦ Uncover the chicken and stir, pressing the lime slices to extract the juice. Microwave on HIGH for 2–3 minutes or until the chicken is tender, stirring occasionally.

♦ Season the chicken with salt, pepper and paprika and leave until cold.

♦ When ready to serve, cut the mango twice lengthways either side of the stone. Scrape the flesh away from the stone and put into a blender or food processor.

♦ Using a teaspoon, scoop out the flesh from one of the mango pieces and put in the blender with the garlic, 30 ml (2 tbsp) cooking liquid from the chicken and the mayonnaise.

♦ Purée until smooth, then season with salt, pepper and paprika. Cut the remaining mango piece into neat cubes and put into a serving bowl.

♦ Remove the chicken from the liquid with a slotted spoon and add to the bowl with the chopped mango.

♦ Pour over the dressing and mix together carefully to coat the chicken.

♦ Tear the salad leaves into small pieces and add to the bowl. Toss together to coat lightly in dressing.

♦ Spoon the salad on to two individual serving plates and sprinkle with the pistachio nuts. Serve immediately.

2 chicken breast fillets, skinned
15 ml (1 tbsp) olive or vegetable oil
1 small lime
salt and pepper
paprika
1 large ripe mango
1 garlic clove, skinned and crushed
30 ml (2 tbsp) mayonnaise
few salad leaves such as endive, radicchio or oak leaf lettuce
15 g (½ oz) blanched pistachio nuts, roughly chopped

MARINATED CHICKEN
WITH PEPPERS AND MARJORAM

SERVES 2

2 chicken breast fillets, skinned
1 garlic clove, skinned and crushed
10 ml (2 tsp) lemon juice
pinch of sugar
45 ml (3 tbsp) olive or vegetable oil
15 ml (1 tbsp) chopped fresh marjoram or 5 ml (1 level tsp) dried
1 small onion, skinned and thinly sliced into rings
salt and pepper
1 small red pepper
1 small yellow pepper
50 g (2 oz) black olives, halved and stoned
15 ml (1 level tbsp) capers
fresh marjoram, to garnish

◆ Cut the chicken breasts in half widthways, and put into a shallow dish just large enough to hold them in a single layer.
◆ Put the garlic, lemon juice and sugar in a small bowl and whisk together. Gradually whisk in the oil. Stir in the marjoram, onion rings, salt and pepper.
◆ Pour over the chicken, cover with cling film and leave to marinate for at least 30 minutes.
◆ Meanwhile, seed the peppers and cut into large chunks. Put into a shallow dish with 30 ml (2 tbsp) water, cover with cling film, pulling back one corner to let steam escape, and microwave on HIGH for 5–6 minutes or until the peppers are just soft, stirring occasionally. Drain and set aside.
◆ To cook the chicken, pull back one corner of the cling film to let steam escape, and microwave on HIGH for 5–6 minutes, or until the chicken is tender, turning once.
◆ Add the peppers, olives and capers and microwave on HIGH for 1–2 minutes or until heated through, stirring once. Serve immediately, garnished with fresh marjoram.

photograph opposite page 81

CHICKEN WITH POTATOES
AND FRESH GINGER

SERVES 1

15 ml (1 tbsp) vegetable oil
1 shallot, skinned and finely chopped
½ small garlic clove, skinned and crushed
1 cm (½ inch) piece fresh root ginger, peeled and finely grated
1.25 ml (¼ level tsp) cumin seeds
1.25 ml (¼ level tsp) coriander seeds
10 ml (2 tsp) tomato purée
100 g (4 oz) potato, cut into 2.5 cm (1 inch) pieces
1 chicken quarter, about 225 g (8 oz), skinned
75 ml (3 fl oz) chicken stock
salt and pepper

◆ Put the oil, shallot, garlic and ginger in a medium bowl. Cover with cling film, pulling back one corner to let steam escape, and microwave on HIGH for 3–4 minutes or until softened, stirring occasionally.
◆ Stir in the cumin, coriander, tomato purée and potato and microwave on HIGH for 2 minutes.
◆ Cut the chicken into two pieces and add to the spice and potato mixture. Stir in the stock and salt and pepper to taste. Mix thoroughly.
◆ Re-cover, and microwave on HIGH for 17–20 minutes or until the chicken is tender, stirring occasionally. Serve hot with a green vegetable.

TO SERVE 2

Double the ingredients.
In Point 1: Put the oil, shallot, garlic and ginger in a large bowl, cover and microwave on HIGH for 5–7 minutes or until softened.
In Point 4: Microwave on HIGH for 25–30 minutes or until the chicken is tender.

LEMON AND MUSTARD MACKEREL

SERVES 1

◆ Put half of the butter and the onion in a small bowl and microwave on HIGH for 3–4 minutes or until the onion has softened, stirring occasionally.

◆ Stir in the breadcrumbs, mustard seeds, the lemon rind and half of the lemon juice and the mustard. Season with salt and pepper and set aside.

◆ Using a sharp knife, bone the mackerel. Cut off the head just behind the gills, then cut along the belly towards the tail so that the fish can be opened out.

◆ Place the fish flat on a board, skin side upwards and with the heel of your hand press along the backbone to loosen it.

◆ Turn the fish over and lift out the backbone, using the tip of a knife to help pull the bone away cleanly.

◆ Discard the bone, then wash and dry the fish. Make three diagonal slashes about 0.5 cm (¼ inch) deep on each side of the fish.

◆ Stuff the fish with the lemon stuffing and put into a shallow dish. Pour over the remaining lemon juice and dot with the remaining butter. Season with salt and pepper.

◆ Cover with cling film, pulling back one corner to let steam escape, and microwave on HIGH for 3–4 minutes or until the fish is tender.

◆ Serve immediately with a little of the cooking liquid poured over. Garnish with lemon slices.

25 g (1 oz) butter or margarine
1 small onion, skinned and finely chopped
40 g (1½ oz) fresh white breadcrumbs
10 ml (2 level tsp) black mustard seeds
finely grated rind and juice of 1 lemon
5 ml (1 level tsp) Dijon mustard
salt and pepper
1 mackerel, weighing about 350 g (12 oz), cleaned
lemon slices, to garnish

TO SERVE 2

Double the ingredients.
In Point 1: Cook for 5–7 minutes or until softened.
In Point 8: Cook for 5–6 minutes or until tender.

SKATE WITH
ANCHOVIES AND CAPERS

SERVES 2

1 small skate wing, weighing about 450 g (1 lb)
50 g (2 oz) butter or margarine
50 g (2 oz) button mushrooms, thinly sliced
half a 50 g (1¾ oz) can anchovy fillets, drained and finely chopped
15 ml (1 level tbsp) capers
pepper
lemon wedges, to garnish

♦ Cut the skate wing in half. Put 25 g (1 oz) of the butter in a large shallow dish and microwave on HIGH for 45 seconds until melted. Arrange the skate in the dish and cover with cling film, pulling back one corner to let steam escape.

♦ Microwave on HIGH for 4 minutes per 450 g (1 lb). Turn the skate over and reposition the pieces halfway through cooking. Remove the skate and place on warmed serving plates.

♦ Add the remaining butter to the dish and microwave on HIGH, uncovered, for 45 seconds, until melted. Add the mushrooms and microwave on HIGH for 1 minute. Add the anchovies and capers and stir well. Microwave on HIGH for 1 minute until hot. Season with pepper. Pour over the skate and serve at once, garnished with lemon wedges.

COD WITH WATERCRESS SAUCE

SERVES 2

1 small bunch of watercress
30 ml (2 tbsp) natural yogurt
5 ml (1 tsp) lemon juice
5 ml (1 level tsp) mild prepared mustard
1 egg yolk
salt and pepper
75 ml (3 fl oz) olive or vegetable oil
2 cod steaks, about 175 g (6 oz) each
15 ml (1 level tbsp) plain flour
15 g (½ oz) butter or margarine

♦ Wash and trim the watercress. Reserve a few sprigs for garnish, and put the rest into a large bowl with 15 ml (1 tbsp) water. Cover with cling film, pulling back one corner to let steam escape, and microwave on HIGH for 1 minute or until the watercress looks slightly limp.

♦ Drain the watercress, let it cool a little, and purée in a blender or food processor with the yogurt, then set aside.

♦ Preheat a browning dish for 8–10 minutes.

♦ Meanwhile, put half of the lemon juice, the mustard, egg yolk, salt and pepper in a medium bowl. Whisk together, then gradually whisk in the oil, a little at a time, until the mixture becomes thick and creamy.

♦ When all the oil has been added, add the remaining lemon juice and more seasoning if necessary. Fold in the watercress purée and set aside.

♦ Lightly coat the fish with the flour and season with salt and pepper. Put the butter into the browning dish, then quickly add the fish.

♦ Microwave on HIGH for 2 minutes, then turn over and microwave on HIGH for 1–2 minutes or until just tender. Transfer to a warmed serving dish.

♦ Microwave the watercress sauce on HIGH for 1 minute or until warm, stirring occasionally. Pour over the fish, garnish with the reserved watercress sprigs and serve immediately.

PASTA, TUNA AND LEMON SALAD

SERVES 1

♦ Put the pasta and salt to taste in a medium bowl and pour over 600 ml (1 pint) boiling water. Stir, then cover with cling film, pulling back one corner to let steam escape. Microwave on HIGH for 6–8 minutes, or until almost tender, stirring occasionally. Leave to stand, covered. Do not drain.

♦ Meanwhile, drain the tuna and put the oil from the can into a medium bowl with the onion. Flake the fish and set aside.

♦ Cover the bowl with cling film, pulling back one corner to let steam escape, and microwave on HIGH for 4–5 minutes, or until the onion is softened, stirring occasionally.

♦ Stir in the cream and the turmeric and microwave on HIGH, uncovered, for 2–3 minutes, until thickened and reduced.

♦ Stir in the lemon rind and juice and season well with salt and pepper.

♦ Drain the pasta, rinse with boiling water and stir into the dressing. Mix thoroughly together.

♦ Stir in the tuna, olives and the parsley. Cover and chill for at least 30 minutes.

♦ To serve, arrange the lettuce on a serving plate and spoon over the salad.

100 g (4 oz) small dried pasta shapes
salt and pepper
100 g (4 oz) can tuna in vegetable oil
1 small onion, skinned and sliced into rings
45 ml (3 tbsp) double cream
pinch of ground turmeric
finely grated rind and juice of ½ lemon
25 g (1 oz) black or green olives
15 ml (1 tbsp) chopped fresh parsley
few lettuce leaves, to serve

TO SERVE 2

Double the ingredients using a 198 g (7 oz) can tuna.

In Point 1: Microwave pasta on HIGH for 8–10 minutes or until just tender.

In Point 3: Microwave the onion on HIGH for 5–7 minutes, or until softened.

In Point 4: Microwave the sauce on HIGH for 3½–4 minutes or until thickened and reduced.

PASTA WITH BOLOGNESE SAUCE

SERVES 2

5 ml (1 tsp) vegetable oil
1 shallot or ½ small onion, skinned and chopped
3 rashers smoked streaky bacon, rinded and chopped
1 garlic clove, skinned and crushed
225 g (8 oz) lean minced beef
1 medium carrot, peeled and grated
1 bay leaf
2.5 ml (½ level tsp) dried oregano
15 ml (1 level tbsp) tomato purée
226 g (8 oz) can tomatoes
150 ml (¼ pint) dry red wine
100 ml (4 fl oz) beef stock
salt and pepper
225 g (4 oz) dried spaghetti

♦ Put the oil, shallot, bacon, garlic and beef in a medium bowl.
♦ Microwave on HIGH for 5–7 minutes or until the onion is soft, and the meat has changed colour, stirring occasionally. Drain off any excess fat.
♦ Stir in the remaining ingredients and cover with cling film, pulling back one corner to let steam escape. Microwave on HIGH for 20–25 minutes or until the meat is tender and the sauce is slightly reduced. Leave to stand.
♦ Meanwhile, put the spaghetti into a large bowl and pour over 1.1 litre (2 pints) boiling water. Stir, cover with cling film, pulling back one corner to let steam escape, and microwave on HIGH for 5–6 minutes, until almost tender. Leave to stand, covered, for 5 minutes. Do not drain.
♦ Microwave the sauce on HIGH for 1–2 minutes, until hot. Drain the spaghetti and turn into a warmed serving dish. Pour the sauce over and serve immediately.

SEAFOOD PASTA

SERVES 2

25 g (1 oz) butter, cut into pieces
15 ml (1 tbsp) vegetable oil
6 medium fresh scallops, shelled
1 medium onion, skinned and finely chopped
1 small garlic clove, skinned and crushed
175 g (6 oz) fresh tagliatelle
salt and pepper
175 g (6 oz) peeled prawns
30 ml (2 tbsp) chopped fresh parsley
150 ml (¼ pint) soured cream
2 whole prawns, lemon or lime slices and parsley sprigs, to garnish

♦ Put the butter and oil in a medium bowl and microwave on HIGH for 45 seconds, until the butter has melted.
♦ Pierce each scallop with the point of a knife and stir into the bowl. Cover with cling film, pulling back one corner to let steam escape, and microwave on HIGH for 1 minute, turning once during cooking.
♦ Remove the scallops from the bowl. Separate the coral from the white flesh and cut the white part into slices.
♦ Add the onion and garlic to the fat remaining in the bowl and microwave on HIGH for 5–7 minutes, or until softened.
♦ Put the tagliatelle and salt to taste in a large bowl. Pour over 1.1 litre (2 pints) boiling water and microwave on HIGH for 3–4 minutes or until almost tender, stirring frequently.
♦ Leave to stand for 2 minutes, then drain and transfer to an ovenproof serving dish. Add the onion mixture, sliced scallops and corals, prawns, parsley, soured cream, salt and pepper.
♦ Toss gently together and microwave on HIGH for 2–3 minutes, until hot. Serve immediately, garnished with the whole prawns, lemon or lime slices and parsley.

SPAGHETTI ALLA CARBONARA

SERVES I

♦ Put the spaghetti and salt to taste in a medium bowl. Pour over 600 ml (1 pint) boiling water. Stir, cover with cling film, pulling back one corner to let steam escape, and microwave on HIGH for 4–5 minutes or until almost tender. Leave to stand, covered. Do not drain.

♦ Meanwhile, put the oil, shallot, garlic and bacon in a medium bowl and cover with cling film, pulling back one corner to let steam escape. Microwave on HIGH for 3–4 minutes or until the onion is soft, stirring occasionally.

♦ Drain the spaghetti and stir into the bacon and onion mixture. Microwave on HIGH for 1 minute or until hot.

♦ Meanwhile, mix the egg, Parmesan, cream, parsley, salt and pepper together.

♦ Quickly pour the egg and cream mixture on to the spaghetti and toss together. Microwave on HIGH for 1 minute, stirring every 15 seconds, until the egg is set. Garnish with parsley and serve immediately with grated Parmesan handed separately.

100 g (4 oz) dried spaghetti
salt and pepper
15 ml (1 tbsp) vegetable oil
1 shallot, skinned and finely chopped
½ small garlic clove, skinned and crushed (optional)
4 rashers streaky bacon, rinded and cut into thin strips
1 egg
30 ml (2 level tbsp) grated Parmesan cheese
30 ml (2 tbsp) double cream
15 ml (1 tbsp) chopped fresh parsley
chopped fresh parsley, to garnish
grated Parmesan cheese, to serve

TO SERVE 2

Double the ingredients.

In Point 1: Put the spaghetti into a large bowl, pour over 1.1 litres (2 pints) boiling water. Stir, cover with cling film, pulling back one corner to let steam escape, and microwave on HIGH for 5–6 minutes or until almost tender.

In Point 2: Microwave the oil, shallot, garlic and bacon on HIGH for 5–7 minutes or until softened, stirring occasionally.

In Point 3: Microwave on HIGH for 1½ minutes or until hot.

In Point 5: Microwave on HIGH for 1–1½ minutes, stirring every 15 seconds, until the egg is set.

CANNELLONI WITH
BROCCOLI AND MIXED NUTS

SERVES 2

6 dried cannelloni tubes
salt and pepper
1 small onion, skinned and chopped
15 ml (1 tbsp) vegetable oil
275 g (10 oz) broccoli, trimmed and finely chopped
finely grated rind and juice of ½ small lemon
50 g (2 oz) chopped mixed nuts, such as Brazilnuts and walnuts
50 g (2 oz) fresh wholemeal breadcrumbs
30 ml (2 level tbsp) grated Parmesan cheese
5 ml (1 tsp) chopped fresh marjoram, or 2.5 ml (½ level tsp) dried
freshly grated nutmeg
1 egg yolk
15 ml (1 level tbsp) plain flour
25 g (1 oz) butter or margarine, cut into pieces
300 ml (½ pint) milk

♦ Put the cannelloni and salt to taste into a large bowl and pour over enough boiling water to cover.

♦ Microwave on HIGH for 5 minutes or until just tender, stirring occasionally. Leave to stand. Do not drain.

♦ Meanwhile, put the onion and oil into a medium bowl, cover with cling film, pulling back one corner to let steam escape, and microwave on HIGH for 3–4 minutes or until softened.

♦ Drain the pasta and spread out on a clean tea towel, cover with a second tea towel or absorbent kitchen paper.

♦ Stir the broccoli and half of the lemon rind and juice into the onion, cover again and microwave on HIGH for 10–12 minutes or until the broccoli is quite soft.

♦ Stir in the nuts, 40 g (1½ oz) of the breadcrumbs, half of the cheese, and the marjoram. Season well with salt, pepper and nutmeg. Stir in the egg yolk.

♦ Use this mixture to stuff the cannelloni, then arrange in two individual shallow gratin dishes. Set aside.

♦ To make the sauce, put the flour, butter, milk and remaining lemon rind and juice in a medium bowl and microwave on HIGH for 5–6 minutes, whisking every 30 seconds, until the sauce thickens.

♦ Season with salt, pepper and nutmeg and pour over the cannelloni.

♦ Microwave on HIGH for 4–5 minutes or until thoroughly heated through.

♦ Sprinkle with the remaining breadcrumbs and cheese and brown under a preheated grill. Serve with a green salad, if liked.

SMOKED HAM AND TOMATO STUFFED AUBERGINES

SERVES 2

♦ Halve the aubergines lengthways. Scoop out the flesh, leaving a shell about 1 cm (½ inch) thick. Put the scooped out flesh into a large bowl and reserve.

♦ Salt the insides of the aubergine shells and leave upside down on a plate for 20–30 minutes, to remove any bitter juices.

♦ Meanwhile, add the oil, onion, garlic, tomatoes, parsley, allspice, green pepper, salt and pepper to the reserved flesh. Microwave, uncovered, on HIGH for 10–12 minutes, until reduced and thickened. Stir in half of the ham and set aside.

♦ Rinse and dry the aubergine halves. Arrange in a circle in a large shallow dish and pour in 150 ml (¼ pint) water, the lemon juice and the sugar.

♦ Cover with cling film, pulling back one corner to let steam escape, and microwave on HIGH for 8–9 minutes or until tender.

♦ Drain the aubergine halves and return to the dish. Spoon in the filling.

♦ Microwave on HIGH for 2–3 minutes or until the filling is hot. Sprinkle with the cheese and the remaining ham and microwave on HIGH for 1 minute or until the cheese has just melted. Serve immediately, garnished with chopped parsley.

2 medium aubergines
salt and pepper
15 ml (1 tbsp) vegetable oil
1 medium onion, skinned and finely chopped
1 garlic clove, skinned and crushed
397 g (14 oz) can tomatoes, drained
30 ml (2 tbsp) chopped fresh parsley
2.5 ml (½ level tsp) ground allspice
1 small green pepper, cored, seeded and chopped
75 g (3 oz) smoked ham, cut into thin strips
15 ml (1 tbsp) lemon juice
5 ml (1 tsp) granulated sugar
75 g (3 oz) Cheddar cheese, grated
chopped fresh parsley, to garnish

VEGETABLE GOULASH

SERVES 1

♦ Put the oil, onion and pepper in a medium bowl. Cover with cling film, pulling back one corner to let steam escape, and microwave on HIGH for 3–4 minutes or until softened, stirring occasionally.

♦ Stir in the paprika and caraway seeds and microwave on HIGH for 1 minute. Stir in the oatmeal and gradually stir in the tomato juice.

♦ Cut the carrot into 0.5 cm (¼ inch) slices and the courgette into 2.5 cm (1 inch) slices. Stir into the paprika mixture and mix well. Season with nutmeg and salt and pepper to taste.

♦ Re-cover and microwave on HIGH for 9–10 minutes or until the vegetables are tender. Serve with the soured cream or yogurt spooned on top, garnished with chopped parsley.

TO SERVE 2

Double the ingredients.
In Point 1: Put the oil, onion and pepper in a large bowl. Cover and microwave on HIGH for 5–7 minutes or until softened.
In Point 4: Microwave on HIGH for 15–20 minutes or until tender.

15 ml (1 tbsp) vegetable oil
1 small onion, skinned and chopped
½ small green pepper, seeded and chopped
10 ml (2 level tsp) sweet paprika
1.25 ml (¼ level tsp) caraway seeds
15 ml (1 tbsp) medium oatmeal
200 ml (7 fl oz) tomato juice
1 medium carrot
1 medium courgette
freshly grated nutmeg
salt and pepper
15 ml (1 tbsp) soured cream or natural yogurt
chopped fresh parsley, to garnish

DINNER *For Two*

BEEF COOKED IN RED WINE

◆

350 g (12 oz) chuck steak
150 ml (¼ pint) dry red wine
1 medium onion, skinned and sliced
1 garlic clove, skinned and crushed
10 ml (2 tsp) chopped fresh oregano or 2.5 ml (½ level tsp) dried
salt and pepper
15 ml (1 tbsp) vegetable oil
3 rashers streaky bacon, rinded and chopped
15 ml (1 level tbsp) plain flour
chopped fresh oregano or parsley, to garnish

◆ Remove any excess fat from the meat and cut into strips 5 cm (2 inches) long and 1 cm (½ inch) wide. Put into a shallow dish and add the wine, onion, garlic, oregano, salt and pepper. Cover and leave in the refrigerator to marinate overnight.

◆ Preheat a browning dish for 8–10 minutes.

◆ Quickly add the oil and bacon and microwave on HIGH for 30 seconds, stirring once.

◆ Remove the meat and onion from the marinade with a slotted spoon and stir into the browning dish. Microwave on HIGH for 2 minutes, stirring once. Stir in the flour and microwave on HIGH for 1 minute.

◆ Gradually stir the marinade and 100 ml (4 fl oz) water into the dish and microwave on HIGH for 4–5 minutes or until the liquid is boiling. Cover with cling film, pulling back one corner to let steam escape, and microwave on MEDIUM for 25–30 minutes, or until tender, stirring occasionally.

◆ Leave to stand for 5 minutes. Adjust the seasoning if necessary, then turn into a warmed serving dish, garnish with oregano and serve.

opposite: Spicy Mini Meatballs with Tomato and Coriander Sauce (see page 63)

STEAK AU POIVRE

♦ Preheat a browning dish for 8–10 minutes.
♦ Using a pestle and mortar, coarsely crush the peppercorns. Spread on a board, then place the steaks on top and press down firmly with the palm of your hand to coat the surface of the meat. Repeat with the other side.
♦ Put the butter and then oil in the browning dish, then quickly add the steaks. Microwave on HIGH for 1 minute, then turn over and microwave on HIGH for 2–3 minutes, or until cooked to taste. Transfer the meat to a warmed serving dish.
♦ Stir the brandy and cream into the cooking juices and microwave on HIGH for 2–3 minutes or until the sauce is reduced and thickened, stirring occasionally. Season with salt, pour over the steaks and serve immediately.

15 ml (1 level tbsp) black peppercorns
2 fillet steaks, about 175 g (6 oz) each
15 g (½ oz) butter or margarine, cut into pieces
15 ml (1 tbsp) vegetable oil
15 ml (1 tbsp) brandy
75 ml (3 fl oz) double cream
salt

CALF'S LIVER WITH APPLE, BACON AND SAGE

♦ Cut the liver into thin strips, trimming away all ducts and gristle. Coat in the flour and season well with salt, pepper and paprika.
♦ Put the oil and the butter into a shallow dish and microwave on HIGH for 30 seconds or until the butter melts.
♦ Meanwhile, cut the bacon into thin strips. Core the apple, cut into rings, then cut each ring in half.
♦ Stir the onion and bacon into the fat and microwave on HIGH for 5–6 minutes, or until the onion is softened, stirring frequently.
♦ Stir in the liver and microwave on HIGH for 1–2 minutes or until the liver just changes colour, stirring occasionally.
♦ Stir in the apple slices and the cider and microwave on HIGH for 2–3 minutes or until the liver is tender, stirring occasionally.
♦ Remove the liver, bacon, apple and onion with a slotted spoon and transfer to a warmed serving dish.
♦ Stir in the remaining cider, the cream and the sage and microwave on HIGH for 4–5 minutes or until thickened and reduced. Adjust the seasoning, if necessary.
♦ Microwave the liver and apple mixture on HIGH for 1 minute to reheat, if necessary, then pour over the sauce. Garnish with sage and serve immediately.

225 g (8 oz) calf's liver, sliced
15 ml (1 level tbsp) plain flour
salt and pepper
paprika
15 ml (1 tbsp) vegetable oil
15 g (½ oz) butter or margarine
3 rashers streaky bacon, rinded
1 red eating apple
1 medium onion, skinned and thinly sliced
200 ml (7 fl oz) medium dry cider
30 ml (2 tbsp) soured cream
5 ml (1 tsp) chopped fresh sage or 2.5 ml (½ level tsp) dried
fresh sage, to garnish

photograph opposite page 96

opposite: Marinated Chicken with Peppers and Marjoram (see page 72)

RACK OF LAMB
WITH MINT AND TAHINI

◆

about 350 g (12 oz) rack of lamb with 6 cutlets, chined
salt and pepper
paprika
freshly grated nutmeg
15 ml (1 tbsp) olive or vegetable oil
75 ml (3 fl oz) chicken stock
1 garlic clove, skinned and crushed
15 ml (1 tbsp) chopped fresh mint or 2.5 ml (½ level tsp) dried
pinch of ground cloves
15 ml (1 tbsp) tahini
1.25 ml (¼ tsp) lemon juice
mint sprigs, to garnish

◆ Preheat a browning dish for 8–10 minutes.

◆ Meanwhile, slash the fat on the lamb at 1 cm (½ inch) intervals and season well with salt, pepper, paprika and nutmeg.

◆ Put the oil in the browning dish, then quickly add the lamb, fat side down, and microwave on HIGH for 2 minutes.

◆ Turn the meat over and microwave on HIGH for 5–6 minutes or until just cooked. The meat should still be pink in the centre. Transfer the meat to a warmed serving dish.

◆ Stir the chicken stock, garlic, mint and the cloves into the dish and mix together, stirring, to loosen any sediment at the bottom of the dish.

◆ Stir in the tahini and lemon juice and season with salt, pepper and paprika. Microwave on HIGH for 1 minute, stirring once.

◆ Slice the lamb into cutlets, spoon over the sauce and serve garnished with mint.

LAMB NOISETTES WITH
ONION AND FRESH SAGE PUREE

◆

15 g (½ oz) butter or margarine, cut into pieces
1 medium onion, skinned and finely chopped
75 ml (3 fl oz) chicken stock
2.5 ml (½ tsp) chopped fresh sage
5 ml (1 tsp) lemon juice
salt and pepper
45 ml (3 tbsp) soured cream
4 lamb noisettes, each about 4 cm (1½ inches) thick
15 ml (1 level tbsp) plain flour
15 ml (1 tbsp) vegetable oil
fresh sage, to garnish

◆ To make the purée, put the butter in a medium bowl and microwave on HIGH for 30 seconds or until melted.

◆ Stir in the onion and cover with cling film, pulling back one corner to let steam escape. Microwave on HIGH for 4–6 minutes or until really soft, stirring occasionally.

◆ Stir in the stock, sage and lemon juice, cover again and microwave on HIGH for 3 minutes, stirring occasionally. Season to taste with salt and pepper. Leave to cool slightly, then add the soured cream.

◆ Preheat a browning dish for 8–10 minutes.

◆ Purée the onion mixture in a blender or food processor, then turn into a clean bowl. Set aside.

◆ Lightly coat the noisettes with the flour and season with salt and pepper. Add the oil to the browning dish, then quickly add the noisettes, arranging them in a circle in the dish. Microwave on HIGH for 2 minutes. Turn over and microwave on HIGH for 1–2 minutes or until cooked as desired. They should still be slightly pink in the centre. Arrange on a warmed serving plate and garnish with fresh sage.

◆ Microwave the onion purée on HIGH for 1–2 minutes or until hot and adjust the seasoning if necessary. Serve immediately with the noisettes.

CINNAMON LAMB WITH
ALMONDS AND APRICOTS

◆

♦ Put the almonds on to a large flat plate and microwave on HIGH for 6 minutes, or until lightly browned, stirring occasionally. Set aside.

♦ Put the apricots into a small bowl and add 150 ml (¼ pint) water. Cover with cling film, pulling back one corner to let steam escape, and microwave on HIGH for 5 minutes. Leave to stand.

♦ Meanwhile, preheat a browning dish for 8–10 minutes.

♦ Meanwhile, cut the lamb into 2.5 cm (1 inch) slices and flatten slightly with a meat mallet or a rolling pin. Cut each slice in half.

♦ Mix the flour, cinnamon, cumin, salt and pepper together and use to coat the meat.

♦ Add the oil to the browning dish, then quickly stir in the meat. Microwave on HIGH for 2 minutes, then turn the meat over and microwave on HIGH for 2 minutes.

♦ Stir in the stock and bay leaf and mix well together. Cover with cling film, pulling back one corner to let steam escape, and microwave on LOW for 10 minutes or until the meat is tender, stirring occasionally.

♦ Drain the apricots and stir into the dish. Microwave on HIGH for 2–3 minutes or until the apricots are hot. Stir in the yogurt and more seasoning if necessary. Serve hot, sprinkled with the toasted almonds.

25 g (1 oz) whole blanched almonds
50 g (2 oz) dried apricots, halved
350 g (12 oz) lamb fillet
15 ml (1 level tbsp) plain flour
10 ml (2 level tsp) ground cinnamon
2.5 ml (½ level tsp) ground cumin
salt and pepper
15 ml (1 tbsp) vegetable oil
75 ml (3 fl oz) chicken stock
1 bay leaf
30 ml (2 tbsp) natural yogurt

ESCALOPES OF PORK IN MUSTARD CREAM SAUCE

◆

15 ml (1 tbsp) vegetable oil
2 thin pork leg steaks, total weight about 350 g (12 oz), rinded
1 shallot or ½ small onion, skinned and finely chopped
100 g (4 oz) mushrooms, sliced
75 ml (3 fl oz) dry white wine
15 ml (1 level tbsp) mild Dijon mustard
75 ml (3 fl oz) single cream
salt and pepper

♦ Preheat a browning dish for 8–10 minutes.
♦ Add the oil, then quickly add the pork and microwave on HIGH for 2 minutes. Turn the escalopes over and microwave on HIGH for 1 minute, then transfer to a warmed serving dish and keep warm.
♦ Stir in the shallot and mushrooms and microwave on HIGH for 3–4 minutes or until softened, stirring occasionally.
♦ Add the wine and microwave on HIGH for 2 minutes or until slightly reduced, then stir in the mustard, cream, salt and pepper and microwave on HIGH for 2 minutes or until reduced and thickened. Pour over the chops and serve immediately.

PORK WITH PINEAPPLE AND GREEN PEPPERCORNS

◆

2 pork loin chops, each about 2.5 cm (1 inch) thick
226 g (8 oz) can pineapple slices in natural juice
5 ml (1 level tsp) cornflour
30 ml (2 tbsp) dry sherry
5–10 ml (1–2 level tsp) green peppercorns
salt
parsley sprigs, to garnish

♦ Preheat a browning dish for 8–10 minutes.
♦ Meanwhile, trim the chops of excess fat and cut the fat into 2.5 cm (1 inch) pieces.
♦ Add the fat to the heated browning dish and microwave on HIGH for 30 seconds or until the fat starts to melt. Quickly add the chops, positioning the thinner ends towards the centre, and microwave on HIGH for 2 minutes. Turn over and microwave on HIGH for 1 minute. Remove the pieces of fat and discard.
♦ Drain the juices from the pineapple can into a bowl, then gradually blend in the cornflour. Stir into the browning dish with the sherry, green peppercorns and salt to taste.
♦ Microwave on HIGH for 5 minutes or until the chops are tender, stirring occasionally.
♦ Add the pineapple rings and microwave on HIGH for 1–2 minutes or until heated through.
♦ To serve, arrange the chops on a warmed serving dish with the pineapple rings and spoon over the cooking liquid. Garnish with parsley.

PORK WITH FRESH PLUM COULIS

◆

◆ Cut the pork into 1 cm (½ inch) slices. Place between sheets of cling film and flatten, using a meat mallet or a rolling pin, to a thickness of 0.5 cm (¼ inch). Set aside.

◆ To make the coulis, put the stock and wine into a medium bowl and microwave on HIGH for 5 minutes or until boiling and slightly reduced.

◆ Reserve one of the plums for the garnish, finely chop the remainder and stir into the hot liquid with the sugar and lemon juice. Cover with cling film, pulling back one corner to let steam escape, and microwave on HIGH for 3–4 minutes or until the plums are tender. Season to taste with salt and pepper.

◆ Allow to cool a little, then purée the coulis in a blender or food processor until smooth, pour back into the bowl and microwave on HIGH for 5–7 minutes or until thickened and reduced.

◆ Put the oil into a shallow dish and microwave on HIGH for 1–2 minutes or until hot. Stir in the pork and microwave on HIGH for 4–5 minutes or until tender, turning once during cooking. Season with salt and pepper.

◆ Reheat the coulis on HIGH for 1–2 minutes or until hot, then spoon on to two warmed serving plates.

◆ Arrange the pork on the sauce, garnish with the reserved plum and the parsley and serve immediately.

350 g (12 oz) pork fillet
50 ml (2 fl oz) chicken stock
50 ml (2 fl oz) fruity white wine
225 g (8 oz) fresh ripe red or purple plums, stoned
15 ml (1 level tbsp) dark brown sugar
5 ml (1 tsp) lemon juice
salt and pepper
15 ml (1 tbsp) vegetable oil
fresh parsley sprigs, to garnish

RED COOKED CHICKEN
WITH LETTUCE CHIFFONADE

◆

2 chicken supremes
5 ml (1 tsp) lemon juice
1 cm (½ inch) piece of fresh root ginger, peeled and finely grated
1 garlic clove, skinned and crushed
5 ml (1 level tsp) garam masala
15 ml (1 level tbsp) paprika
5 ml (1 level tsp) tomato purée
salt and pepper
5 ml (1 level tsp) cornflour
45 ml (3 tbsp) natural yogurt
½ small iceberg lettuce
½ small red pepper, seeded
15 ml (1 tbsp) olive oil

◆ Slash the chicken at 1 cm (½ inch) intervals, using a sharp knife. Put into a small shallow dish. Sprinkle over the lemon juice and set aside.

◆ To make the marinade, mix the ginger, garlic, garam masala, paprika, tomato purée, salt and pepper together. Stir in the cornflour.

◆ Gradually blend in the yogurt to make a thick paste. Spread the paste all over the chicken. Cover and leave to marinate in the refrigerator for 24 hours.

◆ Place the chicken on a microwave roasting rack, arranging the thinner ends towards the centre. Microwave on HIGH for 5 minutes or until tender.

◆ While the chicken is cooking, prepare the chiffonade. Shred the lettuce very finely and arrange on two serving plates. Season with salt and pepper.

◆ Slice the red pepper into very thin strips and arrange on top of the lettuce. Dribble over the olive oil.

◆ Thickly slice the chicken and arrange on top of the chiffonade. Serve hot.

CHICKEN BREASTS
WITH GRUYERE CHEESE

◆

200 ml (7 fl oz) milk
½ small onion, skinned
½ small carrot, sliced
½ celery stick, sliced
1 bay leaf
2 black peppercorns
15 g (½ oz) butter or margarine, cut into small pieces
15 g (½ oz) plain flour
salt and pepper
2 chicken breast fillets, skinned
50 g (2 oz) Gruyère cheese, thinly sliced
chopped fresh parsley, to garnish

◆ Put the milk, onion, carrot, celery, bay leaf and peppercorns in a medium bowl and microwave on HIGH for 3 minutes or until boiling. Leave to infuse for 30 minutes.

◆ Strain the milk and return to the bowl, discarding the flavourings. Add the butter and flour and microwave on HIGH for 2–3 minutes, or until boiling and thickened, whisking frequently. Season with salt and pepper.

◆ Cut each chicken breast in half widthways and put into two individual gratin dishes. Pour over the sauce. Cover with cling film, pulling back one corner to let steam escape, and microwave on HIGH for 4–5 minutes or until the chicken is tender.

◆ Place the sliced cheese on top and microwave on HIGH for 1 minute or until melted. Brown under a preheated grill, if desired. Garnish with parsley and serve hot, straight from the dish.

TURKEY IN SPICED YOGURT

◆

◆ In a medium bowl, mix the spices, yogurt, salt and pepper together. Cut the turkey into 2.5 cm (1 inch) cubes and stir into the spiced yogurt. Cover and leave in the refrigerator to marinate overnight.

◆ Put the oil and onion in a medium bowl, cover with cling film, pulling back one corner to let steam escape, and microwave on HIGH for 3–4 minutes or until softened.

◆ Stir in the coconut and flour and microwave on HIGH for 30 seconds, then gradually stir in the chutney, chicken stock and the turkey and yogurt mixture.

◆ Cover again and microwave on HIGH for 5–6 minutes, or until the meat is tender, stirring occasionally.

◆ Leave to stand for 5 minutes. Adjust the seasoning if necessary, then turn into a warmed serving dish, garnish with parsley and serve immediately.

5 ml (1 level tsp) ground cumin
5 ml (1 level tsp) ground coriander
5 ml (1 level tsp) ground turmeric
2.5 ml (½ level tsp) ground cardamom
150 ml (¼ pint) natural yogurt
salt and pepper
350 g (12 oz) boneless turkey, skinned
15 ml (1 tbsp) vegetable oil
1 small onion, skinned and sliced
30 ml (2 level tbsp) desiccated coconut
15 ml (1 level tbsp) plain flour
15 ml (1 level tbsp) mango chutney
75 ml (3 fl oz) chicken stock
chopped fresh parsley, to garnish

SPICY SPATCHCOCKED POUSSIN WITH GARLIC BUTTER

◆

◆ To make the garlic butter, put the butter into a small bowl and microwave on HIGH for 10–15 seconds or until just soft enough to beat.

◆ Beat in the garlic, salt and pepper. Push to the side of the bowl to form a small pat and chill while cooking the poussin.

◆ Place the poussin on a chopping board, breast side down. Using poultry scissors or a small sharp knife, cut through the backbone to open up the poussin.

◆ Turn the poussin breast side upwards and flatten with a rolling pin. Insert two wooden skewers through the poussin, one through the wings and the breast and one through the drumsticks. These will hold it flat during cooking.

◆ Preheat a browning dish for 8–10 minutes.

◆ Meanwhile, mix together the paprika, cumin, turmeric, tomato purée, lemon juice, chilli sauce and 10 ml (2 tsp) water. Season with salt and pepper, then spread all over the poussin.

◆ Put the oil in the browning dish, then quickly add the poussin, breast side down. Microwave on HIGH for 3 minutes.

◆ Turn over and microwave on HIGH for 8–10 minutes or until tender. Leave to stand for 2–3 minutes.

◆ To serve, remove the skewers, then cut the poussin in half lengthways along the breast. Arrange on two warmed serving plates, spoon over some of the cooking juices and top with the garlic butter. Serve immediately.

25 g (1 oz) butter or margarine
½ small garlic clove, skinned and crushed
salt and pepper
1 poussin, about 700 g (1½ lb)
15 ml (1 level tbsp) paprika
5 ml (1 level tsp) ground cumin
5 ml (1 level tsp) ground turmeric
15 ml (1 level tbsp) tomato purée
10 ml (2 tsp) lemon juice
2.5–5 ml (½–1 tsp) chilli sauce
15 ml (1 tbsp) vegetable oil

CHICKEN WITH
TOMATOES AND OLIVES

◆

15 ml (1 tbsp) vegetable oil
1 medium onion, skinned and chopped
1 garlic clove, skinned and crushed
3 rashers smoked streaky bacon, rinded and chopped
1 green pepper, cored, seeded and chopped
2 chicken thighs, skinned
2 chicken drumsticks, skinned
397 g (14 oz) can tomatoes, drained and chopped
10 ml (2 level tsp) tomato purée
5 ml (1 level tsp) paprika
pinch of sugar
salt and pepper
50 g (2 oz) black olives
30 ml (2 tbsp) chopped fresh parsley
chopped fresh parsley, to garnish

◆ Put the oil, onion, garlic, bacon and green pepper in an ovenproof casserole dish or a large bowl and cover with cling film, pulling back one corner to let steam escape. Microwave on HIGH for 5 minutes or until the vegetables have softened, stirring occasionally.

◆ Add the chicken, tomatoes, tomato purée, paprika, sugar, salt and pepper and microwave on HIGH for 5 minutes or until boiling.

◆ Recover and microwave on HIGH for 15 minutes or until the chicken is tender, turning the chicken over once during cooking and stirring occasionally.

◆ Stir in the olives and parsley and microwave, uncovered, on HIGH for 5 minutes, stirring once. Garnish with chopped parsley and serve hot.

DUCK BREASTS
WITH PORT AND ORANGE

◆

2 duck breast fillets, about 200 g (7 oz) each, skinned
salt and pepper
thinly pared rind and juice of ½ large orange
15 ml (1 tbsp) olive or vegetable oil
15 ml (1 level tbsp) redcurrant jelly
75 ml (3 fl oz) port
pinch of mustard powder
pinch of cayenne pepper
orange twists, to garnish

◆ Preheat a browning dish for 8–10 minutes.

◆ Meanwhile, season the meat with salt and pepper. Cut the pared orange rind into very thin strips.

◆ Add the oil to the browning dish, then quickly put the meat into the dish. Microwave on HIGH for 2 minutes, turn over, stir in the orange strips and juice, redcurrant jelly and the port and microwave on HIGH for 4–5 minutes, or until the meat is tender, turning the duck once.

◆ Remove the duck from the dish. Slice thinly, and arrange on two warmed serving plates.

◆ Stir the mustard and cayenne into the dish and microwave on HIGH for 2–3 minutes or until reduced and thickened. Pour over the duck, garnish with orange twists and serve immediately.

QUAIL WITH
MUSHROOMS AND JUNIPER

◆

◆ Preheat a browning dish for 8–10 minutes. Meanwhile, using a rolling pin, beat each quail 3 or 4 times to flatten slightly.
◆ Add the oil to the dish. Quickly add the quail, breast side down and microwave on HIGH for 2 minutes. Turn over and microwave on HIGH for 1 minute.
◆ Stir in the stock, juniper berries, thyme, mushrooms, salt and pepper and gin. Microwave on HIGH for 6 minutes or until tender, turning the quail once during cooking.
◆ Transfer the quail to a warmed serving dish, then microwave the cooking liquid on HIGH for 3 minutes or until slightly reduced. Season, if necessary, with salt and pepper, then pour over the quail. Garnish with watercress and serve immediately.

photograph overleaf from page 96

4 quail, cleaned
15 ml (1 tbsp) olive or vegetable oil
150 ml (¼ pint) chicken stock
4 juniper berries
2.5 ml (½ level tsp) dried thyme
100 g (4 oz) button mushrooms, sliced
salt and pepper
15 ml (1 tbsp) gin
watercress, to garnish

DUCK IN SWEET AND SOUR SAUCE

◆

◆ Put the duck in a large shallow dish. Cut the orange in half, squeeze the juice from one half and pour over the duck. Cut the other half into slices and reserve for the garnish.
◆ Mix the remaining ingredients with 30 ml (2 tbsp) water and pour over the duck. Cover and leave to marinate for at least 30 minutes, turning once.
◆ Remove the duck from the marinade, leaving the marinade in the dish. Prick the duck skin using a fork. Place the duck, skin side up, on a roasting rack in a large shallow dish. Cover with cling film, pulling back one corner to let steam escape and microwave on HIGH for 5 minutes or until the skin is just starting to brown. Remove from the oven and leave to stand.
◆ Microwave the reserved marinade on HIGH for 2–3 minutes or until boiling, then add the duck portions, skin side down. Cover with cling film, pulling back one corner to let steam escape, and microwave on LOW for 8–10 minutes or until the duck is tender.
◆ Transfer the duck to a serving dish and carve into thick slices. Blend the cornflour to a smooth paste with a little water and stir into the sauce. Microwave on HIGH for 2 minutes until boiling and thickened, stirring occasionally. Spoon over the duck and garnish with the reserved orange slices.

2 duck breast fillets, about 200 g (7 oz) each
1 orange
30 ml (2 tbsp) soy sauce
15 ml (1 level tbsp) soft dark brown sugar
15 ml (1 tbsp) clear honey
15 ml (1 tbsp) red wine vinegar
5 ml (1 tsp) sherry
pinch of ground ginger
salt and pepper

VEAL ESCALOPES
WITH HAM AND MARSALA

◆

1 veal escalope, weighing about 350 g (12 oz)
5 ml (1 tsp) lemon juice
salt and pepper
8 fresh sage leaves
4 thin slices prosciutto
25 g (1 oz) butter or margarine, cut into pieces
15 ml (1 tbsp) vegetable oil
30 ml (2 tbsp) marsala
fresh sage, to garnish

♦ Using a rolling pin, flatten the escalopes between two sheets of greaseproof paper. Cut into four.
♦ Preheat a browning dish for 8–10 minutes.
♦ Meanwhile, sprinkle the escalopes with the lemon juice and season with salt and pepper. Place two sage leaves on each escalope and cover each with a slice of prosciutto. Roll up and secure with a wooden cocktail stick.
♦ Put the butter and the oil into the browning dish, then quickly add the veal. Microwave on HIGH for 2 minutes.
♦ Turn over, reposition and microwave on HIGH for 1 minute, then stir in the marsala and microwave on HIGH for 2–3 minutes or until the meat is tender, stirring occasionally.
♦ Transfer the escalopes to a warmed serving dish and remove the cocktail sticks. Microwave the cooking juices on HIGH for 2–3 minutes or until reduced. Spoon over the escalopes and serve hot, garnished with fresh sage.

TROUT WITH ALMONDS

◆

2 rainbow trout, about 225 g (8 oz) each, cleaned
salt and pepper
15 ml (1 level tbsp) plain flour
15 ml (1 tbsp) vegetable oil
25 g (1 oz) butter or margarine, cut into pieces
25 g (1 oz) flaked almonds
15 ml (1 tbsp) lemon juice
15 ml (1 tbsp) chopped fresh dill

♦ Preheat a browning dish for 8–10 minutes.
♦ Meanwhile, wipe the trout and cut off their heads just behind the gills. Wash and dry with absorbent kitchen paper, then season inside with salt and pepper.
♦ Season the flour with salt and pepper and use to coat the fish.
♦ Put the oil into the browning dish, then quickly add the fish. Microwave on HIGH for 2 minutes, then turn over and microwave on HIGH for 2 minutes, or until the fish is tender.
♦ Transfer the fish to a warmed serving dish and keep warm.
♦ Quickly rinse and dry the browning dish, then add the butter and the almonds and microwave on HIGH for 2–3 minutes or until lightly browned, stirring occasionally.
♦ Stir in the lemon juice, dill, salt and pepper and microwave on HIGH for 1 minute.
♦ Pour the almonds and butter over the trout and serve immediately.

ROULADES OF SOLE WITH SALMON, DILL AND MUSHROOMS

◆

♦ To make the stuffing, drain the salmon, reserving the juice. Remove any skin and large bones. Put the fish into a blender or food processor with 30 ml (2 tbsp) of the cream, the dill, lemon juice, salt and pepper, and process until smooth.

♦ Place the sole fillets, skinned side uppermost, on a board. Score each fillet three or four times with a sharp knife, then spread generously with the stuffing mixture.

♦ Roll up the fillets and secure each with a wooden cocktail stick. Stand upright in a small shallow dish and pour over the reserved salmon juice and the wine.

♦ Cover with absorbent kitchen paper and microwave on LOW for 5–7 minutes or until the fish is tender.

♦ Remove the fish from the cooking liquid with a slotted spoon and arrange on two warmed serving plates.

♦ Microwave the cooking liquid on HIGH for 3–5 minutes or until reduced by half. Stir in the mushrooms, remaining cream, salt and pepper and microwave on HIGH for 2–3 minutes or until the mushrooms are tender.

♦ Microwave the roulades on HIGH, one plate at a time, for 1 minute or until heated through. Spoon over the sauce and garnish with dill sprigs. Serve immediately.

226 g (8 oz) can red salmon
150 ml (¼ pint) double cream
30 ml (2 tbsp) chopped fresh dill or a pinch of dried
10 ml (2 tsp) lemon juice
salt and pepper
4 lemon sole, quarter-cut fillets, skinned
50 ml (2 fl oz) dry white wine
75 g (3 oz) button mushrooms, halved
fresh dill sprigs, to garnish

PARCHMENT BAKED SALMON
WITH CUCUMBER SAUCE

◆

25 g (1 oz) butter or margarine
½ small cucumber, thinly sliced
2 spring onions, finely chopped
60 ml (4 tbsp) dry white wine
10 ml (2 tsp) chopped fresh dill
1.25 ml (¼ level tsp) fennel seeds
salt and pepper
2 salmon steaks, about 175 g (6 oz) each
45 ml (3 tbsp) mayonnaise
30 ml (2 tbsp) natural yogurt
1.25 ml (¼ tsp) lemon juice
fresh dill, to garnish

◆ Put half of the butter in a small bowl and microwave on HIGH for 30 seconds or until melted. Stir in the cucumber slices, reserving six for cooking the salmon, and the spring onions.

◆ Cover with cling film, pulling back one corner to let steam escape, and microwave on HIGH for 4–5 minutes or until tender. Stir in half of the wine and half of the fresh dill, and microwave uncovered on HIGH for 2 minutes. Leave to cool.

◆ Meanwhile, put the remaining butter, the fennel seeds and the remaining wine in a small bowl and microwave on HIGH for 2 minutes or until reduced by half. Season with salt and pepper.

◆ Cut two 28 cm (11 inch) squares of non-stick parchment or greaseproof paper and place a salmon steak on each. Arrange the reserved cucumber slices on top and pour over the butter, wine and fennel seeds. Fold the paper to make two neat parcels.

◆ Place the parcels on an ovenproof plate and microwave on HIGH for 4–5 minutes or until the fish is tender.

◆ While the fish is cooking, finish the sauce. Purée the cooled cucumber and onion mixture in a blender or food processor with the mayonnaise, yogurt, lemon juice, remaining dill, salt and pepper.

◆ Garnish the salmon with dill and serve warm with the cucumber sauce.

photograph overleaf from page 97

SCALLOPS WITH PESTO SAUCE

◆

15 g (½ oz) fresh basil leaves
1 garlic clove, skinned
15 ml (1 level tbsp) pine nuts
25 ml (1 fl oz) olive oil
salt and pepper
15 g (½ oz) Parmesan cheese, grated
30 ml (2 tbsp) double cream
6 large shelled scallops, weighing about 400 g (14 oz)
fresh basil, to garnish

◆ To make the pesto sauce, put the basil, garlic, pine nuts, oil, salt and pepper in a blender or food processor and process until smooth. Fold in the cheese and cream.

◆ Cut the corals from the scallops and set aside. Slice the white part across into 2 discs.

◆ Arrange the white parts in a circle in a large shallow dish. Cover with cling film, pulling back one corner to let steam escape, and microwave on HIGH for 2 minutes or until the scallops are just opaque.

◆ Add the reserved corals and microwave on HIGH for a further 1 minute until the corals are tender.

◆ Drain the scallops, arrange on two plates and spoon over the pesto sauce. Garnish with fresh basil and serve immediately with French bread and a salad, if liked.

MONKFISH BROCHETTES WITH FRESH HERBS

◆

◆ Cut the monkfish into 2.5 cm (1 inch) cubes and put into a medium bowl. Mix together 30 ml (2 tbsp) of the oil, half of the lemon juice, the parsley, tarragon, dill, salt and pepper and pour over the fish.

◆ Cover and leave to marinate in the refrigerator for at least 30 minutes.

◆ Meanwhile, make the sauce. Put the pepper and 75 ml (3 fl oz) water into a medium bowl and cover with cling film, pulling back one corner to let steam escape. Microwave on HIGH for 5–6 minutes or until the pepper is really soft.

◆ Allow to cool a little then put the pepper and cooking liquid in a blender or food processor and blend until smooth. Add the garlic, breadcrumbs, salt and pepper and purée again. Add the remaining oil, drop by drop. Add Tabasco sauce to taste and adjust the seasoning, if necessary. Set aside.

◆ Thread the cubes of monkfish on to six wooden skewers. Arrange in a circle on a large flat plate.

◆ Cover with absorbent kitchen paper and microwave on HIGH for 2–3 minutes, or until the fish is tender, turning once and basting frequently with the marinade during cooking.

◆ Dribble a little of the marinade over the fish and serve hot, with the sauce.

350 g (12 oz) monkfish fillet, skinned
45 ml (3 tbsp) olive or vegetable oil
30 ml (2 tbsp) lemon juice
15 ml (1 tbsp) chopped fresh parsley
10 ml (2 tsp) chopped fresh tarragon
10 ml (2 tsp) chopped fresh dill
salt and pepper
½ small green pepper, cored, seeded and finely chopped
1 small garlic clove, skinned and crushed
45 ml (3 level tbsp) fresh breadcrumbs
few drops Tabasco sauce

WHOLE FISH COOKED WITH GARLIC AND SPICES

◆

◆ Pierce the fish eyes with a sharp knife to prevent them popping during cooking, then slash the fish three times on each side. Set aside.

◆ Put the garlic, lemon rind and juice, chilli, ginger, ground and fresh coriander, garam masala, cardamom, almonds and onion in a blender or food processor and blend until smooth.

◆ Put half of the oil in a medium bowl and stir in the purée. Microwave on HIGH for 2–3 minutes until thickened, stirring occasionally.

◆ Spoon the mixture into the 6 slashes and the inside of the fish.

◆ Place the fish on a large ovenproof serving plate, pour over the remaining oil and season with salt and pepper. Cover loosely with cling film, pulling back one corner to let steam escape, and microwave on HIGH for 4 minutes per 450 g (1 lb) or until tender, turning the fish over once during cooking. Garnish with coriander and serve hot straight from the plate.

1 fish such as sea bass, sea bream or grey mullet, about 700 g (1½ lb), cleaned and scaled if necessary
2 garlic cloves, skinned
finely grated rind and lemon juice
1 green chilli, seeded (optional)
2.5 cm (1 inch) piece fresh root ginger, peeled and finely grated
15 ml (1 level tbsp) ground coriander
30 ml (2 tbsp) chopped fresh coriander
5 ml (1 level tsp) garam masala
2.5 ml (½ level tsp) ground cardamom
15 ml (1 level tbsp) ground almonds
1 medium onion, chopped
30 ml (2 tbsp) vegetable oil
salt and pepper
chopped fresh coriander, to garnish

ACCOMPANIMENTS

VEGETABLES WITH
GINGER AND CASHEW NUTS

SERVES 2

15 ml (1 tbsp) vegetable oil
1 cm (½ inch) piece of fresh root ginger, peeled and grated
pinch of cayenne pepper
25 g (1 oz) unsalted cashew nuts
5 ml (1 level tsp) soft brown sugar
15 ml (1 tbsp) soy sauce
1 small red pepper, cored, seeded and cut into 5 cm (2 inch) strips
100 g (4 oz) button mushrooms, halved
100 (4 oz) beansprouts
salt and pepper

♦ Put the oil, ginger, cayenne pepper and the cashew nuts in a medium bowl and microwave on HIGH for 3–4 minutes, or until lightly browned, stirring frequently.

♦ Remove the cashews from the oil with a slotted spoon and set aside. Stir in the remaining ingredients and mix together well.

♦ Microwave on HIGH for 3–4 minutes, or until the vegetables are just tender, stirring occasionally. Season with salt and pepper, sprinkle with the cashew nuts and serve hot.

SESAME COURGETTES

SERVES 1

♦ Trim the courgettes and cut diagonally into 1 cm (½ inch) slices. Cut each slice lengthways into three.
♦ Put the oil, sesame seeds and garlic, if using, in a medium bowl and microwave on HIGH for 2–3 minutes or until lightly browned, stirring occasionally.
♦ Add the courgettes and the onion to the sesame seeds. Cover with cling film, pulling back one corner to let steam escape, and microwave on HIGH for 2 minutes or until the courgettes are just tender, stirring once. Season with salt and pepper and serve hot.

100 g (4 oz) courgettes
15 ml (1 tbsp) sesame or vegetable oil
15 ml (1 level tbsp) sesame seeds
1 small garlic clove, skinned and crushed (optional)
1 spring onion, trimmed and chopped
salt and pepper

TO SERVE 2

Double all the ingredients except the garlic.
In Point 2: Microwave on HIGH for 3–4 minutes or until lightly browned.
In Point 3: Microwave on HIGH for 3 minutes or until just tender.

CARROTS WITH ORANGE SEGMENTS AND HONEY

SERVES 1

♦ Thinly pare the rind from one third of the orange and cut into very thin strips. Put the strips into a medium bowl.
♦ Remove the remaining rind and pith from the orange. Cut half of the orange into segments and set aside. Squeeze the juice from the remaining half into the bowl with the strips of orange rind.
♦ Cut the carrots into fingers 1 cm (½ inch) wide and 5 cm (2 inches) long. Stir them into the bowl, with the butter. Cover with cling film, pulling back one corner to let steam escape, and microwave on HIGH for 3–4 minutes or until just tender, stirring occasionally.
♦ Uncover and stir in the orange segments, lemon juice, honey, parsley, salt and pepper. Microwave on HIGH for 1 minute or until just heated through, then serve immediately.

1 large orange
75 g (3 oz) carrots, trimmed and scrubbed
knob of butter
5 ml (1 tsp) lemon juice
15 ml (1 tbsp) clear honey
10 ml (2 tsp) chopped fresh parsley
salt and pepper

TO SERVE 2

Double the ingredients.
In Point 1: Pare the rind from half of one of the oranges.
In Point 2: Remove rind and pith from one orange and segment. Squeeze the juice from the other orange.
In Point 3: Microwave on HIGH for 5–7 minutes or until just tender.
In Point 4: Microwave on HIGH for 1–1½ minutes or until just heated through.

BRUSSELS SPROUTS WITH HAZELNUT BUTTER

SERVES 2

25 g (1 oz) hazelnuts
1 shallot or ½ small onion, skinned and finely chopped
25 g (1 oz) butter or margarine
salt and pepper
large pinch of ground cumin
250 g (8 oz) small Brussels sprouts, trimmed

♦ Spread the hazelnuts out evenly on a large flat plate and microwave on HIGH for 2–3 minutes or until the skins 'pop', stirring occasionally.
♦ Rub the skins off, using a clean tea-towel, and chop the nuts finely.
♦ Put the shallot and the butter in a medium bowl and microwave on HIGH for 3–4 minutes or until the shallot is softened, stirring occasionally.
♦ Stir in the hazelnuts and season with salt, pepper and cumin. Microwave on HIGH for 1 minute, then stir in the Brussels sprouts.
♦ Cover with cling film, pulling back one corner to let steam escape, and microwave on HIGH for 4–5 minutes or until just tender, stirring occasionally.

FRENCH BEANS WITH MUSHROOMS

SERVES 2

225 g (8 oz) French beans, trimmed
25 g (1 oz) butter or margarine, cut into pieces
1 garlic clove, skinned and crushed
100 g (4 oz) small button mushrooms, halved
10 ml (2 tsp) mushroom ketchup
10 ml (2 tsp) lemon juice
5 ml (1 tsp) chopped fresh tarragon or 2.5 ml (½ level tsp) dried
salt and pepper
fresh tarragon, to garnish

♦ Cut the beans into 2.5 cm (1 inch) lengths and put into a shallow dish with 30 ml (2 tbsp) water. Cover with cling film, pulling back one corner to let steam escape, and microwave on HIGH for 6 minutes or until just tender, stirring once. Drain and set aside.
♦ Put the butter into a medium ovenproof serving bowl and microwave on HIGH for 45 seconds or until melted. Stir in the garlic, mushrooms, mushroom ketchup and lemon juice and microwave on HIGH for 2 minutes or until the mushrooms are softened, stirring occasionally.
♦ Stir in the tarragon, beans, salt and pepper and microwave on HIGH for 1–2 minutes, or until the beans are heated through. Serve hot, garnished with tarragon.

opposite: Calf's Liver with Apple, Bacon and Sage (see page 81)
overleaf: Quail with Mushrooms and Juniper (see page 89) and Mixed Vegetable Julienne (see page 97)

PETITS POIS A LA FRANCAISE

SERVES 2

♦ Shred the lettuce, removing any thick stalks, and set aside. Put the remaining ingredients and 15 ml (1 tbsp) water into a medium ovenproof serving bowl. Cover with cling film, pulling back one corner to let steam escape, and microwave on HIGH for 5–7 minutes or until the peas are cooked.
♦ Add the shredded lettuce and microwave on HIGH for 30 seconds–1 minute or until warmed through. Serve immediately.

1 lettuce heart
15 g (½ oz) butter or margarine, cut into pieces
450 g (1 lb) fresh peas, shelled
6 spring onions, trimmed and sliced
2.5 ml (½ level tsp) granulated sugar
salt and pepper

MIXED VEGETABLES JULIENNE

SERVES 2

♦ Cut the vegetables into neat strips 5 cm (2 inches) long and 0.5 cm (¼ inch) wide.
♦ Put the butter into a medium ovenproof serving dish and microwave on HIGH for 30 seconds or until melted.
♦ Stir in the vegetables, oregano, lemon juice, salt and pepper and mix together. Cover with cling film, pulling back one corner to let steam escape, and microwave on HIGH for 2–3 minutes or until the vegetables are just tender. Serve immediately.

photograph overleaf from page 96

2 spring onions, trimmed
2 medium carrots, peeled
1 large courgette, trimmed
½ small red, green or yellow pepper, cored and seeded
15 g (½ oz) butter or margarine, cut into pieces
5 ml (1 tsp) chopped fresh oregano or 2.5 ml (½ level tsp) dried
2.5 ml (½ tsp) lemon juice
salt and pepper

overleaf: Parchment Baked Salmon with Cucumber Sauce (see page 92)
opposite: Potato and Leek Ramekins (see page 99) and Cherry Tomatoes with Pine Nut and Basil Dressing (see page 100)

PEPPERS COOKED WITH ONION AND TOMATO

SERVES 2

15 ml (1 tbsp) vegetable oil
1 garlic clove, skinned and crushed
1 medium onion, skinned and thinly sliced
226 g (8 oz) can tomatoes, drained and chopped
5 ml (1 level tsp) tomato purée
1 green pepper, cored, seeded and cut into strips
1 yellow pepper, cored, seeded and cut into strips
5 ml (1 tsp) chopped fresh oregano or 2.5 ml (½ level tsp) dried
salt and pepper

♦ Put the oil, garlic and onion in a medium bowl and cover with cling film, pulling back one corner to let steam escape. Microwave on HIGH for 5–7 minutes or until the onion is softened, stirring occasionally.

♦ Stir in the remaining ingredients and microwave on HIGH for 5 minutes, or until the tomato has reduced to a thick pulp and the peppers are soft, stirring occasionally. Serve hot.

BROCCOLI WITH PARMESAN SAUCE

SERVES 2

15 g (½ oz) butter or margarine, cut into pieces
15 ml (1 level tbsp) plain flour
300 ml (½ pint) milk
salt and pepper
freshly grated nutmeg
30 ml (2 level tbsp) Parmesan cheese, grated
225 g (8 oz) broccoli
Parmesan cheese, to serve (optional)

♦ Put the butter, flour and milk in a medium bowl and microwave on HIGH for 4–5 minutes, until the sauce has boiled and thickened, whisking every minute. Season well with salt, pepper and nutmeg. Stir in the cheese.

♦ Divide the broccoli into small florets and cut the stalks into small pieces. Put the broccoli in a shallow serving dish with 30 ml (2 tbsp) water.

♦ Cover with cling film, pulling back one corner to let steam escape, and microwave on HIGH for 5 minutes or until just tender, stirring occasionally.

♦ Pour over the sauce and microwave on HIGH for 1–2 minutes or until hot. Sprinkle with extra Parmesan, if liked, and serve immediately, straight from the dish.

MANGE-TOUT IN LEMON CREAM DRESSING

SERVES 2

♦ Put the mange-tout into a medium bowl with 15 ml (1 tbsp) water. Cover with cling film, pulling back one corner to let steam escape, and microwave on HIGH for 3–4 minutes or until just tender, stirring once.
♦ Drain and return to the bowl with the remaining ingredients. Microwave on HIGH for 1–2 minutes to heat through, stirring once. Serve immediately.

175 g (6 oz) mange-tout, trimmed
60 ml (4 tbsp) single cream
finely grated rind of 1 small lemon
5 ml (1 tsp) lemon juice
salt and pepper
large pinch of brown sugar
large pinch of ground turmeric

POTATO AND LEEK RAMEKINS

SERVES 2

♦ Grease and line the bases of two 150 ml (¼ pint) ramekin dishes with greaseproof paper.
♦ Prick the potato all over with a fork, place on absorbent kitchen paper and microwave on HIGH for 5–6 minutes or until soft, turning over halfway through cooking.
♦ Meanwhile, finely chop the white part of the leek and slice the green part into very thin 4 cm (1½ inch) long strips. Wash separately and drain well.
♦ Put the white leek into a medium bowl with the milk, cover with cling film, pulling back one corner to let steam escape, and microwave on HIGH for 2–3 minutes or until very soft, stirring occasionally.
♦ Cut the potato in half, scoop out the flesh and stir into the cooked leek and milk. Mash well together and season with salt, pepper and nutmeg. Stir in the egg yolk.
♦ Spoon the mixture into the prepared ramekin dishes. Cover loosely with cling film and microwave on HIGH for 2–2½ minutes or until firm to the touch. Leave to stand.
♦ Meanwhile, put the butter into a small bowl with the strips of green leek and the poppy seeds. Cover with cling film, pulling back one corner to allow steam to escape, and microwave on HIGH for 2–3 minutes or until tender, stirring occasionally. Season with salt and pepper.
♦ Turn the ramekins out on to a warmed serving plate and spoon over the leek and poppy seed mixture. Microwave on HIGH for 1–2 minutes to heat through, if necessary. Serve immediately, with meat or fish.

1 large potato, weighing about 225 g (8 oz)
1 small leek
45 ml (3 tbsp) milk
salt and pepper
freshly grated nutmeg
1 egg yolk
15 g (½ oz) butter or margarine
5 ml (1 level tsp) poppy seeds

photograph opposite page 97

CHERRY TOMATOES WITH PINE NUT AND BASIL DRESSING

SERVES 2

15 ml (1 tbsp) olive or vegetable oil
25 g (1 oz) pine nuts
2.5 ml (½ level tsp) Dijon mustard
2.5 ml (½ level tsp) brown sugar
salt and pepper
2.5 ml (½ tsp) white wine vinegar
225 g (8 oz) cherry tomatoes, cut in halves
15 ml (1 tbsp) chopped fresh basil

♦ Put the oil and the nuts in a medium bowl and microwave on HIGH for 2–3 minutes, or until lightly browned, stirring frequently.
♦ Stir in the mustard, sugar, salt and pepper and whisk together with a fork. Whisk in the vinegar.
♦ Add the tomatoes and microwave on HIGH for 30 seconds, or until the tomatoes are just warm. Stir in the basil and serve immediately.

photograph opposite page 97

CELERIAC AND POTATO PUREE

SERVES 2

225 g (8 oz) celeriac, peeled
1 medium potato, about 175 g (6 oz), peeled
25 g (1 oz) butter or margarine
15 ml (1 tbsp) natural yogurt or milk
salt and pepper
chopped fresh parsley, to garnish

♦ Cut the celeriac and potato into 1.5 cm (¾ inch) cubes. Put into a large shallow dish with 30 ml (2 tbsp) water and cover with cling film, pulling back one corner to let steam escape.
♦ Microwave on HIGH for 8–10 minutes, or until tender, stirring occasionally.
♦ Drain and put into a blender or food processor with the butter, yogurt, salt and pepper and purée until smooth. Return to the dish or turn into a warmed serving dish and microwave on HIGH for 1–2 minutes or until hot. Garnish with parsley and serve immediately.

BAKED NEW POTATOES WITH ORANGE DRESSING

SERVES 2

♦ Prick the potatoes all over with a fork. Arrange in a circle on absorbent kitchen paper on a microwave plate.
♦ Microwave on HIGH for 5–7 minutes, or until the potatoes feel soft, turning them over once during cooking.
♦ Put the butter, orange rind and juice, marmalade, salt and pepper in a small bowl, and microwave on HIGH for 1–2 minutes, or until the butter has melted and the liquid is hot.
♦ Beat in the egg yolk and microwave on LOW for 2–3 minutes, or until thickened, stirring frequently.
♦ Microwave the potatoes on HIGH for 1 minute to reheat, then pour over the sauce. Garnish with orange slices and serve hot.

6 small potatoes, total weight about 350 g (12 oz)
15 g (½ oz) butter, cut into pieces
finely grated rind and juice of ½ orange
5 ml (1 level tsp) orange marmalade
salt and pepper
1 egg yolk
orange slices, to garnish

WARM NEW POTATO SALAD WITH WHOLE GRAIN MUSTARD AND CREAM DRESSING

SERVES 2

♦ Cut the potatoes in half and put into a medium bowl with 60 ml (4 tbsp) water.
♦ Cover with cling film, pulling back one corner to let steam escape, and microwave on HIGH for 5–6 minutes, until just tender, stirring occasionally.
♦ Meanwhile, mix the mustard with the cream, mayonnaise, lemon juice, salt and pepper.
♦ Drain the potatoes and stir into the dressing. Mix together to coat all the potatoes in the dressing. Serve while still warm.

350 g (12 oz) small new potatoes
10 ml (2 level tsp) whole grain mustard
75 ml (3 fl oz) double cream
15 ml (1 tbsp) mayonnaise
5 ml (1 tsp) lemon juice
salt and pepper

BURGHUL PILAU

15 g (½ oz) flaked almonds
15 g (½ oz) butter or margarine
1 medium onion, skinned and finely chopped
1 garlic clove, skinned and crushed
100 g (4 oz) large grained burghul wheat
200 ml (7 fl oz) boiling chicken stock
salt and pepper
30 ml (2 tbsp) natural yogurt
15 ml (1 tbsp) chopped fresh chives or parsley

♦ Put the almonds and butter in a medium bowl and microwave on HIGH for 1–2 minutes or until the almonds are golden brown, stirring occasionally.

♦ Stir in the onion and garlic, cover with cling film, pulling back one corner to let steam escape, and microwave on HIGH for 4–5 minutes, stirring occasionally, until softened.

♦ Meanwhile, wash the burghul wheat in several changes of water. Drain and then stir into the cooked onion and garlic. Stir in the stock, cover again and microwave on HIGH for 6–8 minutes or until tender and all the liquid is absorbed, stirring occasionally.

♦ Season well with salt and pepper, then stir in the yogurt and chives. Serve immediately.

BASMATI RICE WITH PISTACHIO NUTS

100 g (4 oz) Basmati rice
salt and pepper
finely grated rind and juice of 1 lemon
15 g (½ oz) butter or margarine, cut into pieces
15 g (½ oz) blanched pistachio nuts, chopped
15 ml (1 tbsp) chopped fresh parsley

♦ Put the rice, salt to taste, lemon rind and juice and 300 ml (½ pint) boiling water in a medium bowl. Cover with cling film, pulling back one corner to let steam escape, and microwave on HIGH for 7 minutes.

♦ Leave to stand, covered, for 5 minutes by which time the rice should be tender and the liquid absorbed.

♦ While the rice is standing, put the butter into an ovenproof serving dish and microwave on HIGH for 45 seconds or until melted.

♦ Stir the nuts into the butter and microwave on HIGH for 2 minutes, stirring occasionally. Stir in the parsley and season well with salt and pepper.

♦ Gradually stir in the rice, turning carefully with a fork to ensure that all the grains are coated in butter. Add more seasoning, if necessary, and serve hot.

SPICY RED LENTILS WITH COCONUT

SERVES 2

♦ Put the oil, onion and garlic in a large bowl and cover with cling film, pulling back one corner to let steam escape. Microwave on HIGH for 5–7 minutes or until softened, stirring occasionally.

♦ Stir in the cayenne pepper, paprika, cumin and the fennel seeds and microwave on HIGH for 1–2 minutes, stirring frequently. Stir in the lentils.

♦ Mix the creamed coconut with 450 ml (¾ pint) boiling water and stir until the coconut dissolves.

♦ Stir into the spice and lentil mixture. Mix well and microwave on HIGH for 10–15 minutes, stirring occasionally, until the lentils are tender. Add a little extra boiling water during cooking, if needed.

♦ Season with salt and pepper and stir in the coriander, if using. Leave to stand for 5 minutes.

♦ Meanwhile, put the desiccated coconut on a large flat plate and microwave on HIGH for 3–4 minutes or until it feels slightly crispy, stirring frequently.

♦ Reheat the lentils on HIGH for 1–1½ minutes or until warmed through, then turn into a warmed serving dish and sprinkle with the coconut.

15 ml (1 tbsp) vegetable oil
1 medium onion, skinned and finely chopped
1 garlic clove, skinned and crushed
1.25 ml (¼ level tsp) cayenne pepper
5 ml (1 level tsp) paprika
10 ml (2 level tsp) ground cumin
5 ml (1 level tsp) fennel seeds
75 g (3 oz) split red lentils
50 g (2 oz) creamed coconut
salt and pepper
15 ml (1 tbsp) chopped fresh coriander (optional)
15 ml (1 level tbsp) desiccated coconut

FRUITY RICE SALAD

SERVES 2

♦ Put the rice, salt to taste and 300 ml (½ pint) boiling water in a medium bowl. Cover with cling film, pulling back one corner to let steam escape, and microwave on HIGH for 7 minutes.

♦ Leave to stand, covered, for 5 minutes, by which time the rice should be tender and the liquid absorbed.

♦ Meanwhile, finely chop the dates and the spring onions and put into a serving bowl with the sunflower seeds. Put the mustard and honey in a small bowl and, using a fork, gradually whisk in the olive oil. Stir in the vinegar and salt and pepper to taste, then pour over the dates and the onions.

♦ Add the rice and mix together carefully. Leave until cold.

♦ To serve, core and roughly chop the apple and stir into the salad. Serve immediately with meat or fish.

100 g (4 oz) long-grain white rice
salt and pepper
75 g (3 oz) dried dates, stoned
2 spring onions, trimmed
15 ml (1 level tbsp) sunflower seeds
2.5 ml (½ tsp) Dijon mustard
5 ml (1 tsp) clear honey
45 ml (3 tbsp) olive oil
10 ml (2 tsp) white wine vinegar
1 red eating apple

DESSERTS
and Confectionery

PEAR·IN CASSIS

SERVES 1

25 g (1 oz) caster sugar

½ cinnamon stick

1 large ripe pear

15–30 ml (1–2 tbsp) crème de cassis

2.5 ml (½ level tsp) cornflour

few blackcurrants and fresh herb sprigs, to decorate (optional)

langues de chat biscuits, to serve

♦ Put the sugar, cinnamon and 150 ml (¼ pint) water in a medium bowl and microwave on HIGH for 2 minutes or until hot. Stir until the sugar dissolves, then microwave on HIGH for 2 minutes or until boiling.

♦ Meanwhile, peel the pear, cut in half and remove the core.

♦ Place the pear in the hot syrup; cover with cling film, pulling back one corner to let steam escape, and microwave on HIGH for 2–3 minutes or until tender, spooning the syrup over the pears once during cooking.

♦ Remove the pear from the syrup with a slotted spoon and arrange the halves on a warmed serving plate.

♦ Blend the cassis with the cornflour and stir into the syrup. Microwave on HIGH for 1 minute or until thickened, stirring frequently.

♦ Pour the sauce over the pear, decorate with a few blackcurrants and herb sprigs, and serve warm with langues de chat biscuits.

TO SERVE 2

Double the ingredients.

In Point 1: Put the sugar, cinnamon and water in a large bowl and microwave on HIGH for 2½ minutes or until hot. Stir until dissolved, then microwave on HIGH for 2½ minutes or until boiling.

In Point 3: Microwave the pears on HIGH for 3–5 minutes or until tender.

ROSE SCENTED FRUIT SALAD

SERVES 2

♦ Put the sugar in a medium bowl with 150 ml (¼ pint) water. Microwave on HIGH for 2 minutes, then stir until the sugar has dissolved.
♦ Microwave on HIGH for 4 minutes or until slightly reduced, then stir in the lemon juice. Leave until cool.
♦ When the syrup is cool, stir in the prepared fruit and the rose water. Cover and chill for 30 minutes before serving.

50 g (2 oz) granulated sugar
10 ml (2 tsp) lemon juice
1 kiwi fruit, peeled and sliced
100 g (4 oz) black grapes, halved and seeded
2 large oranges, peeled and segmented
5 ml (1 tsp) rose water

WHOLE BAKED NECTARINE

SERVES 1

♦ Put the butter into a medium bowl and microwave on HIGH for 30 seconds or until melted. Add the almonds and oatmeal and microwave on HIGH for 3 minutes or until slightly browned, stirring occasionally. Stir in the honey.
♦ Cut the nectarine in half and remove the stone. Spoon the oatmeal mixture on to the nectarine halves and place in a shallow ovenproof serving dish.
♦ Pour the orange juice into the dish, cover loosely with cling film and microwave on HIGH for 1–1½ minutes or until the nectarine is just soft.
♦ Decorate with toasted flaked almonds and serve warm with the juice spooned over.

15 g (½ oz) unsalted butter
30 ml (2 level tbsp) flaked almonds
15 ml (1 level tbsp) medium oatmeal
5 ml (1 tsp) clear honey
1 large ripe nectarine
juice of ½ small orange
toasted flaked almonds, to decorate

TO SERVE 2

Double the ingredients.
In Point 1: Microwave the butter on HIGH for 45 seconds, or until melted, then stir in the nuts and oatmeal and microwave on HIGH for 4–5 minutes or until lightly browned.
In Point 3: Microwave on HIGH for 1½–2 minutes or until the nectarines are just soft.

BITTER SWEET GRAPES

SERVES 1

175 g (6 oz) grapes, black, green or a mixture of both
finely grated rind and juice of 1 lime
75 ml (3 fl oz) medium white wine
30 ml (2 level tbsp) caster sugar
1 egg, size 6, separated
shredded lime rind, blanched, to decorate (optional)

◆ Halve and seed the grapes and put into a serving bowl. Cover and chill.

◆ Meanwhile, put the lime rind and juice into a small bowl with the wine and 15 ml (1 level tbsp) of the caster sugar.

◆ Microwave on HIGH for 1 minute or until the sugar has dissolved and the liquid is boiling.

◆ Microwave on HIGH for 3–3½ minutes or until the syrup has reduced by half. Do not stir.

◆ When ready to serve, put the egg yolk and remaining sugar in a medium bowl. Whisk well together, then gradually whisk in 15 ml (1 tbsp) of the syrup. Pour the remaining syrup over the grapes.

◆ Microwave the egg yolk mixture on HIGH for 30 seconds. Whisk again, then microwave on HIGH for 1 minute, whisking every 15 seconds or until foamy and thickened.

◆ Whisk the egg white until it just holds its shape, then fold into the egg yolk mixture. Decorate with the grated lime rind and serve immediately with the grapes.

TO SERVE 2

Double all the ingredients.

In Point 3: Microwave on HIGH for 2–3 minutes or until the sugar is dissolved and the liquid is boiling.

In Point 4: Microwave on HIGH for 6–8 minutes or until the liquid is reduced by half. Do not stir.

In Point 5: Use 30 ml (2 tbsp) of the syrup.

In Point 6: Microwave on HIGH for 45 seconds. Whisk, then microwave on HIGH for 1–1½ minutes, whisking every 20 seconds or until foamy and thickened.

HOT STUFFED DATES

SERVES 2

♦ Mix together the almonds, pistachio nuts, ginger and cinnamon. Stir in the honey and mix well.
♦ Stuff the dates with this mixture and arrange on a small ovenproof plate.
♦ Cover loosely with cling film and microwave on HIGH for 1–1½ minutes or until hot. Leave to stand.
♦ Meanwhile, make the sauce. Put the cream and the rum into a heatproof jug. Mix well together and microwave on HIGH for 3 minutes or until thickened and reduced.
♦ Pour the sauce around the dates, decorate and serve immediately.

TO SERVE 2

Double all the ingredients.
In Point 3: Cook for 2–3 minutes or until hot.
In Point 4: Cook for 5–7 minutes or until reduced.

photograph opposite page 113

15 ml (1 level tbsp) ground almonds
15 ml (1 level tbsp) chopped pistachio nuts
small pinch ground ginger
large pinch ground cinnamon
15 ml (1 tbsp) clear honey
3 large fresh dates, pitted
45 ml (3 tbsp) double cream
2.5 ml (½ tsp) rum
3 pistachio nuts, split, to decorate

LEMON GATEAU SLICE

SERVES 2

♦ Line the bases of two 11×7.5 cm (4½×3 inch), 350 ml (12 fl oz) ovenproof containers with greaseproof paper.
♦ Put the butter into a medium bowl and microwave on HIGH for 15 seconds or until just soft enough to beat.
♦ Stir in the flour, sugar, salt, egg and lemon rind and beat until smooth.
♦ Spoon into the prepared containers. Cover with absorbent kitchen paper and microwave on HIGH for 1–2 minutes or until the cakes are risen but still look slightly moist on the surface. Turn the cakes once during cooking.
♦ Leave to stand for 5 minutes, then turn out and leave to cool on a wire rack.
♦ Meanwhile, make the filling. Beat the cheese, cream and icing sugar together with half of the lemon juice.
♦ When the cakes are cool, spread one with 15 ml (1 tbsp) of the lemon curd.
♦ Spread half of the cream cheese mixture on top of the lemon curd, then sandwich the two cakes together.
♦ Swirl the remaining cream cheese mixture on top of the cake.
♦ Put the remaining lemon curd and the remaining lemon juice in a small bowl and microwave on HIGH for 10 seconds, until just melted but not hot. Beat together, then drizzle on top of the cake to make a decorative pattern. Cut the gâteau in half to serve.

50 g (2 oz) butter or margarine, cut into pieces
50 g (2 oz) self-raising flour
50 g (2 oz) soft light brown sugar
pinch of salt
1 egg, beaten
finely grated rind and juice of ½ lemon
75 g (3 oz) low fat soft cheese
30 ml (2 tbsp) single cream
15 ml (1 level tbsp) icing sugar
30 ml (2 tbsp) lemon curd

BAKED CLEMENTINE CUSTARDS

SERVES 2

2 clementines or satsumas
25 ml (1½ level tbsp) caster sugar
15 ml (1 tbsp) orange-flavoured liqueur (optional)
200 ml (7 fl oz) milk
1 egg and 1 egg yolk

◆ Finely grate the rind of one of the clementines. Put half into a heatproof jug with 10 ml (½ level tbsp) of the sugar and 75 ml (3 fl oz) water.

◆ Microwave on HIGH for 2 minutes or until boiling, then continue to boil on HIGH for 2 minutes. Leave to cool.

◆ Peel and segment the fruit, remove the pips and stir the fruit into the syrup with the liqueur, if using. Set aside to cool completely.

◆ Mix the remaining rind and sugar with the milk, egg and egg yolk. Beat well together, then pour into two 150 ml (¼ pint) ramekin or soufflé dishes.

◆ Cover loosely with cling film, then microwave on LOW for 8–10 minutes or until the custards are set around the edge but still soft in the centre.

◆ Leave to stand for 20 minutes. When cool, chill for at least 2 hours.

◆ To serve, decorate each custard with a few marinated clementine segments and serve the rest separately.

◆ 1The custards will keep for up to one day in the refrigerator, so they can be served for two meals.

IF SERVING 1

The custards will keep for up to one day in the refrigerator, so they can be served for two meals.

ALMOND AMARETTI TRIFLES

SERVES 2

100 ml (4 fl oz) milk
1 egg
10 ml (2 level tsp) granulated sugar
1 drop vanilla flavouring
50 g (2 oz) Amaretti biscuits, crushed
30 ml (2 tbsp) orange juice
15 ml (1 tbsp) Amaretti or dry sherry
75 g (3 oz) strawberries
15 g (½ oz) flaked almonds

◆ Put the milk in a heatproof jug and microwave on HIGH for 1–1½ minutes or until hot, but not boiling.

◆ Whisk the egg and sugar together, add the milk, mix well and strain back into the jug. Microwave on LOW for 1½–2 minutes or until the custard just coats the back of a spoon, whisking frequently. Stir in the vanilla flavouring. Cover the surface of the custard with cling film or damp greaseproof paper and leave until cold.

◆ Meanwhile, divide the biscuits between two individual glass serving dishes. Mix the orange juice and sherry together and pour over the biscuits. Leave to stand until the custard is cold.

◆ When the custard is cold, slice the strawberries, reserving two for decoration. Arrange the sliced strawberries on top of the biscuits, then pour over the custard. Chill for at least 30 minutes before serving.

◆ To serve, put the almonds on a large flat plate and microwave on HIGH for 6–8 minutes or until lightly browned, stirring occasionally.

◆ Sprinkle the almonds on top of the trifles and decorate each with a reserved whole strawberry.

SUMMER PUDDING

SERVES 2

♦ Cut the crusts off the bread and cut the bread slices into neat fingers. Reserve about a quarter and use the rest to line the base and sides of two 150 ml (¼ pint) ramekin dishes, making sure that there are no spaces between the bread.

♦ Hull the strawberries and put into a medium bowl with the raspberries.

♦ Sprinkle with the sugar and add 45 ml (3 tbsp) water. Cover with cling film, pulling back one corner to let steam escape, and microwave on HIGH for 5–7 minutes or until the sugar dissolves, the juices begin to flow and the fruit softens.

♦ Reserve about 45 ml (3 tbsp) of the juice and pour the remaining fruit and juice into the lined ramekins. Cover with the reserved bread.

♦ Place a small saucer with a weight on it on top of each pudding and refrigerate overnight.

♦ To serve, turn out on to two serving plates and spoon over the reserved juice. Serve with whipped cream.

5–6 thin slices of day old white bread
150 g (5 oz) strawberries
150 g (5 oz) raspberries
45 ml (3 level tbsp) granulated sugar
whipped cream, to serve

DARK CHOCOLATE MOUSSE WITH PALE CHOCOLATE SAUCE

SERVES 2

♦ Break 50 g (2 oz) of the plain chocolate into small pieces and put into a medium bowl. Microwave on LOW for 5–7 minutes or until just melted. Beat in the egg yolk.

♦ Put the coffee and 15 ml (1 tbsp) hot water in a small bowl. Sprinkle over the gelatine and microwave on LOW for 1–1½ minutes or until the gelatine is dissolved, stirring occasionally. Stir into the chocolate mixture.

♦ Whisk half of the cream until stiff and fold into the chocolate mixture.

♦ Whisk the egg white until stiff and fold into the chocolate mixture.

♦ Pour into two 13×9.5 cm (5×4 inch) base lined containers. Leave in a cool place to set.

♦ To make the sauce, break the remaining chocolate into small pieces and put into a small bowl. Microwave on LOW for 2–3 minutes or until just melted.

♦ Stir the remaining cream and the cocoa into the melted white chocolate and microwave on HIGH for 1 minute or until hot. Leave until cold, stirring occasionally.

♦ To serve, spoon the sauce on to two flat plates. Unmould the mousse, cut in half and arrange one half on each plate. Decorate with a few strawberries, and serve immediately.

75 g (3 oz) plain chocolate
1 egg, separated
2.5 ml (½ level tsp) instant coffee granules
2.5 ml (½ level tsp) gelatine
150 ml (¼ pint) double cream
5 ml (1 level tsp) cocoa powder
few strawberries, to decorate (optional)

APRICOT CHEESECAKES

SERVES 2

100 g (4 oz) Ricotta or curd cheese
1 egg yolk
30 ml (2 level tbsp) ground almonds
30 ml (2 level tbsp) caster sugar
finely grated rind of ½ lemon
20 ml (4 tsp) brandy
400 g (14 oz) can apricot halves in natural juice
15 ml (1 level tbsp) apricot jam
mint sprigs, to decorate

photograph opposite page 112

◆ Put the Ricotta cheese and egg yolk into a medium bowl and beat thoroughly together.

◆ Beat in the almonds, sugar and lemon rind. Gradually stir in 10 ml (2 tsp) of the brandy.

◆ Drain the apricots, reserving the juice. Finely chop one apricot half and stir into the cheese mixture.

◆ Spoon into two 150 ml (¼ pint) ramekin dishes and level the surface. Cut two of the apricot halves crossways into thin slices and fan out. Press lightly on top of the cheesecakes.

◆ Microwave on LOW for 15 minutes, or until slightly shrinking away from the edges. Leave to stand for 10 minutes, then chill.

◆ Meanwhile, purée the remaining apricots and 30 ml (2 tbsp) of the juice in a blender or food processor. Pour into a small bowl and stir in the remaining brandy.

◆ Microwave on HIGH for 2 minutes or until boiling. Leave to cool.

◆ To serve, unmould the cheesecakes and put on to two serving plates. Put the apricot jam into a small bowl and microwave on HIGH for 30 seconds or until melted. Brush the cheesecakes with the glaze.

◆ Pour the sauce around the cheesecakes and decorate with the mint.

SUMMER STRAWBERRY SORBET

SERVES 2

40 g (1½ oz) sugar
225 g (8 oz) strawberries, halved
finely grated rind and juice of ½ orange
1 egg white, size 6
strawberries or crisp biscuits, to decorate

◆ Put the sugar and 60 ml (4 tbsp) water into a heatproof jug and microwave on HIGH for 3–4 minutes or until boiling.

◆ Stir until the sugar has dissolved. Microwave on HIGH for 4–5 minutes or until reduced to a syrup. Do not stir.

◆ Meanwhile, push the strawberries through a fine sieve using the back of a wooden spoon. Stir in the orange rind and juice.

◆ Allow the syrup to cool slightly, then stir into the strawberry purée.

◆ Pour into a shallow freezer container, cover and freeze for 1–1½ hours or until just mushy.

◆ Remove from the freezer, turn into a bowl and beat well with a fork to break down the ice crystals.

◆ Whisk the egg white until stiff and fold into the sorbet.

◆ Pour back into the freezer container and freeze for about 2 hours, until firm.

◆ To serve, microwave on HIGH for 15–20 seconds to soften slightly. Serve decorated with strawberries or crisp biscuits, if liked.

FRESH MINT ICE CREAM

SERVES 2

♦ Put the sugar and 100 ml (4 fl oz) water in a medium bowl. Microwave on HIGH for 3 minutes or until boiling, stirring occasionally.

♦ Stir until the sugar is completely dissolved, then microwave on HIGH for 2 minutes. Leave to cool slightly.

♦ Pull the mint leaves from the stems and put into a blender or food processor. Pour in the syrup and blend until smooth. Strain through a sieve. Stir in the lemon juice. Leave to cool completely.

♦ Whip the cream until just standing in peaks, then fold into the mint mixture.

♦ Pour into a shallow container, cover and freeze for about 30 minutes or until firm around the edge.

♦ Mash with a fork to break down the ice crystals, then freeze for 1 hour or until firm. Serve garnished with mint sprigs and Pale Chocolate Sauce, if liked.

50 g (2 oz) caster sugar
1 large bunch of mint, about 25 g (1 oz)
30 ml (2 tbsp) lemon juice
150 ml (¼ pint) double cream
mint sprigs, to decorate
Pale Chocolate Sauce, to serve (see page 109)

BREAD AND BUTTER PUDDING

SERVES 2

♦ Thickly spread the bread with the butter. Cut each slice into four fingers and arrange half in a deep 600 ml (1 pint) flameproof dish.

♦ Sprinkle with the fruit, half of the sugar and half of the cinnamon.

♦ Top with the remaining bread, buttered side uppermost and sprinkle with the remaining sugar and cinnamon.

♦ Beat the egg and milk together and pour over the bread. Leave for about 20 minutes so that the bread absorbs some of the liquid.

♦ Microwave, uncovered, on LOW for 15 minutes or until just set.

♦ Leave to stand for 5 minutes. Cook under a preheated grill until brown, then serve hot.

3 large slices of bread, crusts removed
25 g (1 oz) butter
40 g (1½ oz) currants or sultanas
15 ml (1 level tsp) caster sugar
1.25 ml (¼ level tsp) ground cinnamon
1 egg
200 ml (7 fl oz) milk

BANANA AND PASSION FRUIT UPSIDEDOWN PUDDING

SERVES 2

25 g (1 oz) butter or margarine
25 g (1 oz) soft light brown sugar
25 g (1 oz) self raising wholemeal flour
1.25 ml (¼ level tsp) ground mixed spice
1 egg, beaten
1 medium ripe banana
15 ml (1 tbsp) clear honey
1 ripe passion fruit

◆ Line the base of an 7.5×11 cm (3×4½ inch) ovenproof dish with greaseproof paper.
◆ Put the butter into a medium bowl and microwave on HIGH for 10–15 seconds or until just soft enough to beat.
◆ Add the sugar, flour, mixed spice and the egg and beat well together using a wooden spoon, until the mixture is well blended and slightly glossy.
◆ Cut half the banana into thin slices and arrange in the base of the prepared dish.
◆ Mash the remaining banana and stir into the sponge mixture. Beat together well.
◆ Spoon the mixture on top of the banana slices and cover with a double thickness of absorbent kitchen paper.
◆ Microwave on MEDIUM for 4–4½ minutes or until slightly shrunk away from the sides of the dish, but the surface still looks wet.
◆ Leave to stand, covered, for 5 minutes, then turn out on to a serving plate.
◆ Put the honey in a ramekin dish or cup. Halve the passion fruit and spoon the pulp into the dish with the honey. Microwave on HIGH for 15–30 seconds or until warmed through. Spoon over the pudding and serve warm.

FRUIT DUMPLINGS WITH SOURED CREAM

SERVES 2

15 g (½ oz) butter or margarine
10 ml (2 level tsp) soft light brown sugar
1 egg yolk
5–10 ml (1–2 tsp) milk
50 g (2 oz) plain wholemeal flour
2.5 ml (½ level tsp) ground mixed spice
freshly grated nutmeg
2 firm ripe plums
15 ml (1 level tbsp) caster sugar
1.25 ml (¼ level tsp) ground cinnamon
15 ml (1 level tbsp) finely chopped walnuts (optional)
75 ml (3 fl oz) soured cream, to serve

◆ Put the butter into a medium bowl and beat until soft. Stir in the brown sugar, egg yolk and milk and beat well. Stir in the flour, mixed spice and nutmeg to taste, and mix to make a fairly stiff dough, adding more milk if necessary.
◆ Turn the dough on to a floured board and knead until smooth. Roll out the dough thinly and stamp out four rounds using an 8.5 cm (3½ inch) fluted cutter.
◆ Halve and stone the plums. Place a plum half on two of the pastry rounds. Mix the caster sugar and the cinnamon together and sprinkle half of it on the plums. Place the remaining plum halves on top.
◆ Dampen the edges of the remaining dough rounds and place firmly on top of the plums, pressing together to seal the edges.
◆ Arrange the dumplings on either side of a buttered dish. Cover with cling film, pulling back one corner to let steam escape, and microwave on HIGH for 1–2 minutes or until just firm to the touch, turning once during cooking.
◆ Leave to stand for 5 minutes, then sprinkle with the remaining cinnamon sugar and the chopped walnuts, if using. Serve warm with soured cream.

opposite: Apricot Cheesecake (see page 110)

RUM TRUFFLES

MAKES ABOUT 12

◆ Break the chocolate into small pieces and put into a medium bowl with the butter. Microwave on LOW for 3–4 minutes, until melted.
◆ Stir well together, then stir in the cake crumbs, icing sugar and rum.
◆ Cover and refrigerate for about 30 minutes or until the mixture is firm.
◆ Lightly dust your fingers with icing sugar and roll the truffle mixture into 12 small balls, then roll each one in the cocoa powder or chocolate vermicelli to coat completely.
◆ Put into petit four cases and chill in the refrigerator until required. If storing overnight, cover with cling film.
◆ To serve, remove from the refrigerator 30 minutes before serving. Serve with coffee instead of dessert, or as a between meal treat.

50 g (2 oz) plain chocolate
25 g (1 oz) unsalted butter
50 g (2 oz) trifle sponge cakes, crumbled
25 g (1 oz) icing sugar, plus extra for dusting
5–10 ml (1–2 tsp) dark rum
25 g (1 oz) cocoa powder or chocolate vermicelli

CHOCOLATE, FRUIT AND NUT SLICES

MAKES 12 SLICES

◆ Spread the hazelnuts out evenly on a large flat plate and microwave on HIGH for 2–3 minutes, or until the skins 'pop', stirring occasionally.
◆ Rub the skins off using a clean tea towel and chop the nuts finely.
◆ Put the chocolate and butter in a medium bowl and microwave on LOW for 4–5 minutes or until melted.
◆ Meanwhile, put the biscuits into a polythene bag and crush finely using a rolling pin.
◆ Stir the crushed biscuits, hazelnuts, cherries, raisins, mixed peel and Tia Maria into the chocolate mixture. Mix well together.
◆ Cover, and refrigerate for about 30 minutes or until the mixture is firm enough to handle.
◆ Turn the mixture out on to a sheet of greaseproof paper and shape into a sausage about 25.5 cm (10 inches) long.
◆ Wrap up tightly in the paper, twisting the ends to keep the shape.
◆ Chill for at least 1 hour or until required.
◆ Unwrap, sift the icing sugar on top and then roll in the icing sugar. Cut into 1.5 cm (¾ inch) slices to serve.

40 g (1½ oz) hazelnuts
50 g (2 oz) plain chocolate, broken into small pieces
75 g (3 oz) unsalted butter
25 g (1 oz) rich tea biscuits
50 g (2 oz) glacé cherries, finely chopped
30 ml (2 level tbsp) raisins
15 ml (1 level tbsp) chopped mixed peel
10 ml (2 tsp) Tia Maria
30 ml (2 level tbsp) icing sugar

opposite: Hot Stuffed Dates (see page 107)

RICE PUDDING

SERVES 1

15 ml (1 level tbsp) sugar

45 ml (3 level tbsp) short-grain pudding rice

knob of butter or margarine

300 ml (½ pint) milk

freshly grated nutmeg

♦ Put the sugar, rice, butter and milk into a medium bowl and mix thoroughly together. Add freshly grated nutmeg to taste.
♦ Microwave on HIGH for 5 minutes or until boiling, stirring occasionally. Microwave on LOW for 17–20 minutes or until the rice is soft, stirring occasionally. Serve hot or cold sprinkled with extra grated nutmeg, if liked.

TO SERVE 2

Double the ingredients.
In Point 2: Microwave on HIGH for 8 minutes or until boiling, stirring occasionally. Microwave on LOW for 35–40 minutes or until the rice is soft, stirring occasionally.

BANANAS WITH HONEY AND ORANGE

7 g (¼ oz) butter or margarine

15 ml (1 tbsp) clear honey

1.25 ml (¼ level tsp) mixed spice

1 large orange

1 medium banana, peeled

♦ Put the butter, honey and mixed spice in a medium bowl or heatproof serving dish. Microwave on HIGH for 30 seconds or until the butter is just melted.
♦ Stir in the finely grated orange rind and juice of half of the orange, peel the other half and cut into chunks. Cut the banana into 2.5 cm (1 inch) pieces and stir into the honey mixture.
♦ Microwave on HIGH for 1–2 minutes or until the bananas are just hot, stirring occasionally. Serve immediately with thick natural yogurt or ice cream.

TO SERVE 2

Double the ingredients.
In Point 1: Microwave on HIGH for 45 seconds or until butter is just melted.
In Point 3: Microwave on HIGH for 2–3 minutes.

APPLE CAKES

SERVES 2

♦ Roughly chop the apple and divide between two 150 ml (¼ pint) ramekin dishes. Sprinkle with half of the cinnamon and the sultanas and mix together. Cover loosely with cling film and microwave on HIGH for 2 minutes, or until the apple is slightly softened.

♦ Meanwhile, beat the butter, sugar, flour and eggs together, using a wooden spoon, until the mixture is well blended and slightly glossy.

♦ Spoon the mixture on top of the apples and level the surfaces. Microwave on HIGH for 2–3 minutes or until slightly shrunk away from the sides of the dishes, but the surface still looks wet.

♦ Leave to stand, covered, for 5 minutes then turn out on to two serving plates.

♦ Mix the remaining cinnamon with the icing sugar and sieve over the cakes. Serve immediately with thick natural yogurt or cream.

1 medium eating apple, peeled and cored
2.5 ml (½ level tsp) ground cinnamon
10 ml (2 tsp) sultanas
25 g (1 oz) butter or margarine
25 g (1 oz) caster sugar
25 g (1 oz) self-raising wholemeal flour
1 egg, size 6
2.5 ml (½ level tsp) icing sugar

TURKISH DELIGHT

MAKES ABOUT 12 SQUARES

vegetable oil
75 g (3 oz) granulated sugar
25 g (1 oz) cornflour, plus extra for dusting
5 ml (1 level tsp) gelatine
few drops of rose water or peppermint essence
few drops of red or green food colouring
15 g (½ oz) icing sugar

◆ Lightly oil a 13×9.5 cm (5×4 inch) ovenproof container. Dust generously with cornflour.

◆ Put the sugar and 100 ml (4 fl oz) water in a medium bowl and microwave on HIGH for 2 minutes, or until hot but not boiling. Stir until the sugar has dissolved.

◆ Blend the gelatine with 50 ml (2 fl oz) water and set aside. Stir half the cornflour into the sugar syrup. Microwave on HIGH for 1–2 minutes, or until the mixture is very thick, stirring every minute. Stir in the gelatine mixture, rose water or peppermint essence to taste and red or green food colouring to give a pale colour.

◆ Spoon the mixture into the container and leave in the refrigerator for about 2 hours, until set.

◆ Sift the remaining cornflour and the icing sugar on to a sheet of greaseproof paper. Turn the Turkish delight out on to it and cut into 12 squares.

◆ Coat all the cut surfaces of the squares with the cornflour mixture and leave, uncovered, for about 4 hours or until the surface of the Turkish delight is dry.

◆ Store for up to 2 weeks in an airtight container with any remaining sugar and cornflour mixture.

WHITE CHOCOLATE COLETTES

MAKES 8

75 g (3 oz) white chocolate
15 g (½ oz) butter
5 ml (1 tsp) brandy
30 ml (2 tbsp) double cream
crystallised violets, to decorate

◆ Arrange eight petit four cases on a plate.

◆ Break 50 g (2 oz) of the chocolate into small pieces and put into a small bowl. Microwave on LOW for 3–5 minutes or until just melted, stirring occasionally.

◆ Spoon a little chocolate into each paper case and, using a clean paint brush, coat the inside of each case with chocolate. Leave for about 30 minutes or until set.

◆ Microwave the chocolate remaining in the bowl on LOW for 1–2 minutes or until just melted, then repeat the coating process, making sure that the chocolate forms an even layer.

◆ Leave for about 30 minutes in a cool place to set completely, then carefully peel away the paper from the chocolate cases.

◆ Break the remaining chocolate into small pieces and add to the bowl with the butter. Microwave on LOW for 3–5 minutes or until just melted, stirring occasionally. Stir in the brandy. Leave for about 10 minutes, until cool but not set. Whisk thoroughly.

◆ Whisk in the cream. Leave for about 5–10 minutes or until thick enough to pipe.

◆ Spoon into a piping bag fitted with a small star nozzle and pipe into the chocolate cases. Decorate each with a crystallised violet. Leave to chill in the refrigerator for at least 1 hour.

◆ Store in the refrigerator until ready to eat. Arrange the colettes in clean paper cases and serve after dinner with coffee.

GLOSSARY

ARCING This happens when a dish or utensil made of metal, or with any form of metal trim or decoration, is used in the microwave. The metal reflects the microwaves and produces a blue spark, this is known as arcing. If this happens the oven should be switched off immediately because arcing can damage the oven magnetron.

ARRANGING FOOD Arranging food in a circle with the centre left empty, will provide the best results when cooking in a microwave, because the 'hole' left in the centre provides a greater area of outer edges for the microwaves to penetrate. Unevenly shaped food should be arranged with the thinner parts towards the centre.

BROWNING DISH Browning dishes are made of a special material which absorbs microwave energy. They are heated empty in the microwave oven for 8–10 minutes, or according to the manufacturers instructions, during which time they get very hot. The food is then placed on the hot surface and is immediately seared and browned.

COVERING FOOD Cling film, roasting bags, absorbent kitchen paper or a lid are all suitable for covering food in the microwave. Cling film and roasting bags should be pierced or slit to allow the build-up of steam to escape during cooking. Roasting bags should be tied with non-metalic ties.

CLEANING It is important to clean the oven interior each time it is used as any spillage will absorb microwave energy and slow down the cooking next time you use the oven. Cleaning is easy, just wipe with a damp cloth.

MICROWAVE
TERMS

DENSITY A dense food such as meat will take longer to defrost, reheat or cook than porous, light and airy foods such as bread, cakes and puddings because microwaves cannot penetrate as deeply into denser, heavier foods.

FOIL It is safe to use very smooth pieces of foil to protect less dense parts of food which would otherwise cook more quickly than the thicker parts. However, if there is any sign of arcing the oven should be switched off and the foil removed immediately. Foil is also useful for covering food during standing time to keep heat in.

GRILL Foods such as gratins which do not brown in the microwave may be browned under a preheated grill after cooking. Remember to cook the food in a flameproof dish and not a microwave container if you intend to do this.

PRICKING Foods with a skin or membrane, such as whole fish, egg yolks and jacket potatoes, should be pricked or slashed to prevent them bursting during cooking.

POWER OUTPUT This refers to the wattage of the oven. Refer to your manufacturer's handbook to find the power output of your oven.

RE-ARRANGING Foods such as meatballs may be re-arranged during cooking. Move food from the outside of the dish towards the centre, and those from the centre to the outside of the dish.

ROTATING Foods which cannot be stirred, such as large cakes or joints of meat, may be given a quarter-turn three times during cooking.

STANDING TIME Food continues to cook after it has been removed from a microwave oven, or when the microwave energy has been switched off. It is no longer being cooked by microwave energy but by the conduction of heat towards the centre. The period during which this happens is known as the 'standing time' and is sometimes necessary to complete the cooking process.

STIRRER Some microwave ovens have a built in 'stirrer' positioned behind a splatter guard or cover in the roof of the cavity. This has the same effect as a turntable and it circulates the microwaves evenly throughout the oven.

STIRRING Since the outer edges of food normally cook first in a microwave oven, stir from the outside of the dish towards the centre to produce an evenly cooked result.

TEMPERATURE PROBE/FOOD SENSOR A temperature probe enables you to control cooking by the internal temperature of the food, rather than by time. The probe is inserted into the thickest part of the food being cooked and the desired temperature selected. When the internal temperature reaches the pre-set level, the oven switches itself off.

THAWING When thawing in a microwave it is essential that the ice is melted slowly, so that the food does not begin to cook on the outside before it is completely defrosted through to the centre. To prevent this happening, food must be allowed to 'rest' between bursts of microwave energy. A DEFROST setting does this automatically by pulsing the energy on and off, but it can be done manually if your oven does not have an automatic defrost control.

FRESH VEGETABLES

Note: All times are given as a guide only, since variations in size and quality will affect cooking times. Add 15 ml (1 tbsp) water and cover unless otherwise stated.

VEGETABLES need very little water added when microwaved. In these charts 15 ml (1 tbsp) water was added and then the dish was covered, unless otherwise stated. In this way, they retain their colour, flavour and nutrients more then they would if cooked conventionally. Cook the vegetables in a large shallow dish with thicker parts towards edge of dish; cook on HIGH/ 100%. They can also be cooked in boil-in-the-bags; plastic containers and polythene bags – make sure there is a space for steam to escape. Prepare vegetables in the normal way. It is most important that food is cut to an even size and stems are of the same length. Vegetables with skins, such as aubergines, need to be pierced before microwaving to prevent bursting. Season vegetables with salt after cooking; salt distorts the microwave patterns and dries the vegetables.

VEGETABLE	QUANTITY	APPROXIMATE TIME ON HIGH SETTING	MICROWAVE COOKING TECHNIQUE(S)
ARTICHOKE, GLOBE	1 2	5–6 Minutes 7–8 Minutes	Place upright in covered dish.
ASPARAGUS	225 g/8 oz	5–6 Minutes	Place stalks towards the outside of the dish. Re-position during cooking.
BEANS, BROAD	225 g/8 oz	3–4 Minutes	Stir or shake.
BEANS, GREEN (Sliced into 2.5 cm/1 inch lengths)	225 g/8 oz	5 Minutes	Stir or shake during the cooking period. Time will vary with age of beans.
BROCCOLI (Small florets)	225 g/8 oz	5–6 Minutes	Re-position during cooking.
BRUSSELS SPROUTS	225 g/8 oz	4–6 Minutes	Stir or shake during cooking.
CABBAGE (Shredded)	225 g/8 oz	5 Minutes	Stir or shake during cooking.
CARROTS (Sliced)	225 g/8 oz	3–4 Minutes	Stir or shake during cooking.
CAULIFLOWER (Florets)	225 g/8 oz	5–6 Minutes	Stir or shake during cooking.
CELERY (2.5 cm/1 inch lengths)	225 g/8 oz	6 Minutes	Stir or shake during cooking.
CORN-ON-THE-COB	two (450 g/ 1 lb)	6–7 Minutes	Wrap individually in greased greaseproof paper. Do not add water. Turn over after 3 Minutes. ▶

COURGETTES (1 cm/½ inch slices)	225 g/8 oz	3–4 Minutes	Stir or shake gently twice during cooking. Stand for 1 minute before draining.
FENNEL (Thinly sliced)	225 g/8 oz	4–5 Minutes	Stir or shake during cooking.
LEEKS (1 cm/½ inch slices)	225 g/8 oz	4 Minutes	Use 30 ml (2 tbsp) water. Stir or shake during cooking.
MANGE TOUT	225 g/8 oz	2 Minutes	Stir or shake during cooking.
BUTTON MUSHROOMS (Whole)	225 g/8 oz	2–3 Minutes	Do not add water. Add 25 g (1 oz) butter and a squeeze of lemon juice. Stir or shake during cooking.
ONIONS (Thinly sliced)	225 g/8 oz	7–8 Minutes	Stir or shake during cooking.
OKRA	225 g/8 oz	3 Minutes	Stir or shake during cooking.
PARSNIPS (Halved, if large)	225 g/8 oz	5–6 Minutes	Place thinner parts towards the centre. Add a knob of butter and 7.5 ml (½ tbsp) lemon juice with 30 ml (2 tbsp) water. Turn dish during cooking and re-position.
PEAS	225 g/8 oz	4–5 Minutes	Stir or shake during cooking.
POTATOES Baked Jacket	one 175 g/ 6 oz potato	4–5 Minutes	Wash and prick the skin with a fork. Place on absorbent kitchen paper or napkin. Turn over half way through cooking.
	two 175 g/ 6 oz potato	6–8 Minutes	
BOILED (OLD) (2.5 cm/1 inch cubes)	225 g/8 oz	3–4 Minutes	Add 30 ml (2 tbsp) water. Stir or shake during cooking.
BOILED (NEW) (Halved)	225 g/8 oz	3 Minutes	Do not overcook or new potatoes become spongy.
SWEET	225 g/8 oz	2–3 Minutes	Wash and prick the skin with a fork. Place on absorbent kitchen paper. Turn over halfway through cooking time.
SWEDE/ TURNIP (2.5 cm/1 inch cubes)	225 g/8 oz	4 Minutes	Stir or shake during cooking.

BECAUSE meat does not brown on the outside when cooked in a microwave, it is important to follow cooking times exactly and to allow the meat to stand, tented in foil, for the required time to guarantee that the meat is ready. Start roasting meat fatty side down and turn it over half way through the cooking time. To help meat to brown, baste it with unsalted butter during cooking; elevating the joint high in the oven also helps browning, as do roasting bags.

TYPE	TIME/SETTING	TECHNIQUE(S)
	BEEF	
BONED ROASTING JOINT (sirloin, topside)	per 450 g (1 lb) Rare: 5–6 minutes on HIGH Medium: 7–8 minutes on HIGH Well: 8–10 minutes on HIGH	*Turn* joint over halfway through cooking time. *Stand* for 15–20 minutes tented with foil.
ON THE BONE ROASTING joint (fore rib, back rib)	per 450 g (1 lb) Rare: 5 minutes on HIGH Medium: 6 minutes on HIGH Well: 8 minutes on HIGH	*Shield* bone end with small piece of foil during first half cooking time. *Turn* joint over halfway through cooking time. *Stand* as for boned joint.
	LAMB/VEAL	
BONED ROLLED JOINT (loin, leg, shoulder)	per 450 g (1 lb) Medium: 7–8 minutes on HIGH Well: 8–10 minutes on HIGH	*Turn* joint over halfway through cooking time. *Stand* as for beef.
ON THE BONE (leg and shoulder)	per 450 g (lb) Medium: 6–7 minutes on HIGH Well: 8–9 minutes on HIGH	*Shield* as for beef. *Position* fatty side down and turn over halfway through cooking time. *Stand* as for beef.
CHOPS	1½ minutes on HIGH then 1½–2 minutes on MEDIUM	*Cook* in preheated browning dish, or finish off under grill. *Position* with bone ends towards centre.

▶

TYPE	TIME/SETTING	TECHNIQUE(S)
	PORK	
BONED ROLLED JOINT (loin, leg)	8–10 minutes on HIGH per 450 g (1 lb)	As for boned rolled lamb above.
ON THE BONE (leg, hand)	8–9 minutes on HIGH per 450 g (1 lb)	As for lamb on the bone above.
CHOPS	1 chop: 4–4½ minutes on HIGH 2 chops: 5–5½ minutes on HIGH 3 chops: 6–7 minutes on HIGH 4 chops: 6½–8 minutes on HIGH	*Cook* in preheated browning dish, or finish off under grill. *Position* with bone ends towards centre. *Cover* kidney, if attached, with greaseproof paper. *Stand* for 2 minutes for 1 chop, 3–5 minutes for 2–4 chops.
SAUSAGES	2 sausages: 2½ minutes on HIGH 4 sausages: 4 minutes on HIGH	*Pierce* skins. *Cook* in preheated browning dish or finish off under grill. *Turn* occasionally during cooking.
	BACON	
JOINTS	12–14 minutes on HIGH per 450 g (1 lb)	*Cook* in pierced roasting bag. *Turn* joint over partway through cooking time. *Stand* for 10 minutes, tented in foil.
RASHERS	2 rashers: 2–2½ minutes on HIGH 4 rashers: 4–4½ minutes on HIGH 6 rashers: 5–6 minutes on HIGH 12 minutes on HIGH per 450 g (1 lb)	*Arrange* in a single layer. *Cover* with greaseproof paper to prevent splattering. *Cook* in preheated browning dish if preferred. *Remove* paper immediately after cooking to prevent sticking. For large quantities: *Overlap* slices and place on microwave rack. *Reposition* three times during cooking. ►

TYPE	TIME/SETTING	TECHNIQUE(S)
	OFFAL	
LIVER (lamb and calves)	6–8 minutes on HIGH per 450 g (1 lb)	*Cover* with greaseproof paper to prevent splattering.
KIDNEYS	8 minutes on HIGH per 450 g (1 lb)	*Arrange* in a circle. *Cover* to prevent splattering. *Reposition* during cooking.
TONGUE	20 minutes on HIGH per 450 g (1 lb)	*Reposition* during cooking.

POULTRY

ALWAYS ensure that frozen poultry is completely thawed before cooking. Large chickens and turkeys will brown if cooked in roasting bags. However, poultry portions will not brown because of the short length of time required to cook them, but they can be browned under the grill when cooking is complete.

TYPE	TIME/SETTING	TECHNIQUE(S)
	CHICKEN	
WHOLE CHICKEN	8–10 minutes on HIGH per 450 g (1 lb)	*Cook* in a roasting bag, breast side down and turn halfway through cooking. *Brown* under conventional grill, if preferred. *Stand* for 10–15 minutes.
WHOLE POUSSIN	5 minutes on HIGH	*Cook* in a pierced roasting bag. *Turn* over as for whole chicken.
PORTIONS	6–8 minutes on HIGH per 450 g (1 lb)	*Position* skin side up with thinner parts towards centre. *Reposition* halfway through cooking time. *Stand* for 5–10 minutes.
BONELESS BREAST	2–3 minutes on HIGH	*Brown* under grill, if preferred.

▶

TYPE	TIME/SETTING	TECHNIQUE(S)
DUCK		
WHOLE	7–10 minutes on HIGH per 450 g (1 lb)	*Turn* over as for whole chicken. *Stand* for 10–15 minutes.
PORTIONS	4×300 g (11 oz) pieces: 10 minutes on HIGH, then 30–35 minutes on MEDIUM	*Position* and *reposition* as for chicken portions above.
TURKEY		
WHOLE	9–11 minutes on HIGH per 450 g (1 lb)	*Turn* over 3–4 times, depending on size, during cooking; start cooking breast side down. *Stand* for 10–15 minutes.
BONELESS ROLL	10 minutes on HIGH per 450 g (1 lb)	*Turn* over halfway through cooking time.

FISH

Fish cooks superbly in a microwave, retaining its natural flavour and juice particularly well. To prevent fish from drying, brush with unsalted butter and cover during cooking. The skin of whole fish should be slashed to prevent it from bursting during cooking. When cooking more than one fish, overlap the thin parts to prevent them from cooking too quickly, and keep them separate with small pieces of cling film or greaseproof paper.

TYPE	TIME/SETTING	TECHNIQUE(S)
WHOLE ROUND FISH (whiting, mullet, trout, carp, bream, small haddock)	3 minutes on HIGH per 450 g (1 lb)	*Slash* skin to prevent bursting. *Turn* over fish partway through cooking time. *Shield* tail with small pieces of smooth foil. *Reposition* fish if cooking more than 2.

◄

TYPE AND QUANTITY	TIME/SETTING	TECHNIQUE(S)
WHOLE FLAT FISH (plaice, sole)	3 minutes on HIGH	*Slash* skin. *Turn* dish partway through cooking time. *Shield* tail as for round fish.
CUTLETS, STEAKS, FILLETS	4 minutes on HIGH per 450 g (1 lb)	*Position* thicker parts towards outside overlapping thin ends and separating with cling film. *Turn* over fillets and quarter-turn dish 3 times during cooking.
SMOKED FISH	4 minutes on HIGH per 450 g (1 lb)	Follow techniques for type of fish above.

A LTHOUGH there are no real time savings to cooking rice and pasta in the microwave, it may be a more foolproof way of cooking as there is no risk of their sticking to the pan. Standing is necessary to complete cooking.

RICE AND PASTA

TYPE	TIME/SETTING	TECHNIQUE(S)
WHITE LONG GRAIN RICE 225 g (8 oz)	10–12 minutes	*Stir* once during cooking. *Stand* for 10 minutes.
BROWN RICE, 100 g (4 oz)	30 minutes	As for white long grain.
PASTA SHAPES, 225 g (8 oz) dried	7 minutes	*Stir* once during cooking. *Stand* for 5 minutes.
SPAGHETTI, TAGLIATELLE, 225 g (8 oz) dried	7–8 minutes	*Stand* for 10 minutes.

I N D E X

A

Almond amaretti trifles 108
Apples:
Apple and banana spread 23
Apple cakes 115
Date and apple porridge 15
Apricots:
Apricot cheesecakes 110
Apricot jam 21
Aubergines:
Aubergine purée with red pepper and pitta bread 39
Smoked ham and tomato stuffed aubergines 79
Avocado and prawns, hot 37

B

Bacon:
To cook bacon 10, 11
Bacon and egg 17
Scampi and bacon kebabs 54
Warm bacon and cabbage salad with mustard dressing 25
Baguette sandwich with salami and red pepper sauce, hot 37
Bananas:
Apple and banana spread 23
Banana and passionfruit upside-down pudding 112
Bananas and honey and orange 114
Basmati rice with pistachio nuts 102
Beans, French:
French bean and Brazil nut salad with blue cheese dressing 25
French beans with mushrooms 96
Beef:
Beef cooked in red wine 80
Beef with ginger and garlic 60
Chilli con carne 62
Cottage pie 61
Spicy mini meatballs with tomato and coriander sauce 63
Steak and kidney pudding 62
Steak au poivre 81
Bitter sweet grapes 106
Bread:
Bread and butter pudding 111
Gruyère and caraway bread 41
Lemon and herb bread 41
Sesame bread 45
Breakfasts, cooking 10–11
Brie with celery and apple salad, warm 26
Broccoli:
Broccoli with Parmesan sauce 98
Cannelloni with broccoli and mixed nuts 78
Browning foods 8, 10, 13
Brussels sprouts with hazelnut butter 96
Burgers, spicy nut 48
Burghal pilau 102
Buttermilk and dill soup 44

C

Cabbage:
Warm bacon and cabbage salad with mustard dressing 25
Cake:
Lemon gâteau slice 107
Cannelloni with broccoli and mixed nuts 78
Carrots with orange segments and honey 95
Celeriac and potato purée 100
Cheese:
Baked potato with cheese and fresh herbs 39

Blue cheese dressing 25
Cheese and salami pie 31
Cheese in vine leaves 50
Gruyère and caraway bread 41
Hot cheese mousse with green peppercorns 32
Melted cheese and ham sandwich 35
Parmesan mushrooms 38
Parmesan sauce 98
Cheesecakes, apricot 110
Cherry tomatoes with pine nut and basil dressing 100
Chicken:
To brown chicken 10
Chicken and curried mayonnaise 59
Chicken and potatoes and fresh ginger 72
Chicken breasts with Gruyère cheese 86
Chicken, mango and pistachio nut salad 71
Chicken tacos 43
Chicken with tomatoes and olives 88
Coronation chicken 26
Herby chicken parcel 70
Marinated chicken with peppers and marjoram 72
Red cooked chicken with lettuce chiffonade 86
Shredded chicken with mushrooms and poppyseeds 70
Chicken livers:
Chicken liver pâté with garlic and Melba toast 30
Warm spinach and chicken liver salad with croûtons 52
Chick peas with tomatoes and chilli 36
Chilli con carne 62
Chocolate:
Chocolate, fruit and nut slices 113
Dark chocolate mousse with pale chocolate sauce 109
White chocolate colettes 116
Chowder, smoked haddock 45
Cinnamon lamb with almonds and apricots 83
Cleaning oven 7, 9
Clementine custards, baked 108
Cling film, use of 8, 10
Club sandwich 43
Cod:
Cod with watercress sauce 74
Fish stuffed courgettes with tarragon sauce 53
Containers 9–10
Coronation chicken 26
Cottage pie 61
Courgettes:
Chilled courgette mousse with saffron sauce 46
Fish stuffed courgettes with tarragon sauce 53
Sesame courgettes 95
Covering dishes 13
Croûtons 52
Custards, baked clementine 108

D

Dates:
Date and apple porridge 15
Hot stuffed dates 107
Devilled kidneys 19
Dinners, cooking 11
Dolmas, lettuce, with tomato sauce 49
Duck:
Duck breasts with port and orange 88

Duck in sweet and sour sauce 89
Dumplings, fruit, with soured cream 112

E

Eggs:
To cook 10–11
Bacon and egg 17
Creamy scrambled egg with smoked salmon 16
French toast 18
Mushroom soufflé omelette 31
Oeuf en cocotte 16
Poached eggs on a muffin 17
Tarragon egg on a pasta nest 29
Escalopes of pork in mustard cream sauce 84

F

Fish see Cod etc.
Fish terrine with basil sauce 55
Whole fish cooked with garlic and spices 93
French beans see Beans, French
French toast 18
Fruit see Apples etc.
Fruit compôte with yogurt 15
Fruit dumplings with soured cream 112
Fruity rice salad 103
Poached fruit 14
Rose-scented fruit salad 105

G

Garlic butter 87
Goulash, vegetable 79
Granary leek toasts 35
Granola, crunchy breakfast 23
Grapes, bitter sweet 106
Gruyère and caraway bread 41

H

Haddock:
Fish stuffed courgettes with tarragon sauce 53
Smoked haddock chowder 45
Smoked haddock kedgeree 18
Ham:
Melted cheese and ham sandwich 35
Hazelnut butter 96
Herby chicken parcel 70
Herring roes with grapes, soft 27
Herrings in oatmeal 19

I

Ice cream, fresh mint 111

J

Jam, apricot 21

K

Kebabs, scampi and bacon 54
Kedgeree:
To reheat 11
Smoked haddock kedgeree 18
Kidneys:
Devilled kidneys 19
Kidneys and mushrooms in red wine 69
Kidneys Indienne in pitta bread 40
Steak and kidney pudding 62

L

Lamb:
Cinnamon lamb with almonds and apricots 83
Indian spinach and lamb curry 64
Lamb chops with rosemary and garlic 63
Lamb noisettes with onion and fresh sage purée 82
Minted lamb burgers with cucumber 65
Rack of lamb with mint and tahini 82
Leeks:
Granary leek toasts 35
Potato and leek ramekins 99
Lemons:
Lemon and herb bread 41
Lemon and mustard mackerel 73
Lemon cream dressing 99
Lemon gâteau slice 107
Lentils:
Lentil, mint and yogurt salad 38
Spicy lentil soup 24
Spicy red lentils with coconut 103
Lettuce dolmas with tomato sauce 49
Lime curd 21
Liver:
Calf's liver with apple, bacon and sage 81
Lunches, cooking 11

M

Mackerel, lemon and mustard 73
Mange tout in lemon cream dressing 99
Marmalade, orange 22
Meat see Beef etc.
To cook 8, 9
Meatballs:
To cook 8
Spicy mini meatballs with tomato and coriander sauce 63
Microwaves, action of 7–8
Mint ice cream, fresh 111
Monkfish:
Monkfish and mange tout sauté 54
Monkfish brochettes with fresh herbs 93
Moussaka 64
Mushrooms:
French beans with mushrooms 96
Hot mushroom mousse with hollandaise sauce 47
Kidneys and mushrooms in red wine 69
Mushrooms on toast 20
Mushroom soufflé omelette 31
Parmesan mushrooms 38
Prawn and mushroom scallops 57
Mussels in cream and garlic sauce 58

N

Nectarine, whole baked 105
Noodles with goat's cheese and chives 28
Nut burgers, spicy, with coriander raita 48

O

Oeuf en cocotte 16
Orange marmalade 22

P

Parchment baked salmon with cucumber sauce 92
Parmesan mushrooms 38
Passionfruit:
Banana and passionfruit upside-down pudding 113
Pasta:
Cannelloni with broccoli and mixed nuts 78
Noodles with goat's cheese and chives 28
Pasta, tuna and lemon salad 75

Pasta with Bolognese sauce 76
Seafood pasta 76
Sea shells with anchovy and parsley dressing 57
Spaghetti alla carbonara 77
Tagliatelle with fresh figs 28
Tarragon egg on a pasta nest 29
Pâté, chicken liver, with garlic and Melba toast 30
Pear in cassis 104
Pepperoni and baked bean snack 42
Peppers:
Pepper and ginger soup with sesame bread 45
Peppers cooked with onion and tomato 98
Stuffed peppers and tomatoes 50
Petits pois à la Française 97
Pilau, burghal 102
Piperade 34
Pizza, vegetarian wholemeal 33
Plaice:
Fish terrine with basil sauce 55
Stuffed plaice timbales with lemon herb butter 56
Pork:
Escalopes of pork with mustard cream sauce 84
Marinated pork with peanuts 67
Pork with blackcurrant sauce 68
Pork with fresh plum coulis 85
Pork with horseradish cream sauce 67
Pork with pineapple and green peppercorns 84
Spare ribs with redcurrant and honey glaze 66
Porridge:
To reheat 11
Date and apple porridge 15
Potatoes:
Baked new potatoes with orange dressing 101
Baked potato with cheese and fresh herbs 39
Celeriac and potato purée 100
Potato and leek ramekins 99
Potato pancakes 20
Warm new potato salad with mustard and cream dressing 101
Poussin, spicy spatchcocked, with garlic butter 87
Power output 12–13
Prawns:
Hot avocado and prawns 37
Prawn and mushroom scallops 57
Prawn and sesame parcels with beansprout salad 42
Prawns and lettuce cooked in brandy and cream 27
Spicy butterfly prawns 55

Q

Quail, stuffed, with mushrooms and juniper 89

R

Raspberries:
Summer pudding 109
Reheating foods 9
Rice:
Basmati rice with pistachio nuts 102
Fruity rice salad 103
Rice pudding 114
Smoked haddock kedgeree 18
Roasting bags, use of 10
Rose-scented fruit salad 105
Rotating foods 8
Roulades of sole with salmon, dill and mushrooms 91
Rum truffles 113

S

Safety aspects 7
Salmon, parchment baked, with cucumber sauce 92
Salt, use of 9
Sausages, cooking 11
Scallops with pesto sauce 92
Scampi and bacon kebabs 54
Seafood pasta 76
Sea shells with anchovy and parsley dressing 57
Sesame bread 45
Sesame courgettes 95
Settings, oven 12–13
Skate with anchovies and capers 74
Sole:
Fish terrine with basil sauce 55
Roulades of sole with salmon, dill and mushrooms 91
Sorbet, summer strawberry 110
Soup:
Buttermilk and dill soup 44
Pepper and ginger soup 45
Smoked haddock chowder 45
Spicy lentil soup 24
Spaghetti:
Pasta with Bolognese sauce 76
Spaghetti alla carbonara 77
Spare ribs with redcurrant and honey glaze 66
Spinach:
Spinach tarts with tomato and basil salad 51
Warm spinach and chicken liver salad with croûtons 52
Steak and kidney pudding 62
Steak au poivre 81
Stew, cooking 11
Strawberries:
Summer pudding 109
Summer strawberry sorbet 110
Summer pudding 109
Summer strawberry sorbet 110
Suppers, cooking 11

T

Tagliatelle:
Seafood pasta 76
Tagliatelle with fresh figs 28
Tarragon egg on a pasta nest 29
Thawing food 9
Tomatoes:
Cherry tomatoes with pine nut and basil dressing 100
Stuffed peppers and tomatoes 50
Tomato and basil salad 51
Trout with almonds 90
Tuna:
Pasta, tuna and lemon salad 75
Tuna fish 32
Turkey in spiced yogurt 87
Turkish delight 116

V

Veal escalopes with ham and Marsala 90
Vegetables, mixed:
Mixed vegetables julienne 97
Vegetable goulash 79
Vegetables with ginger and cashew nuts 94

W

Whiting:
Fish terrine with basil sauce 55